New Wave English Skills Practice

B

Revised edition

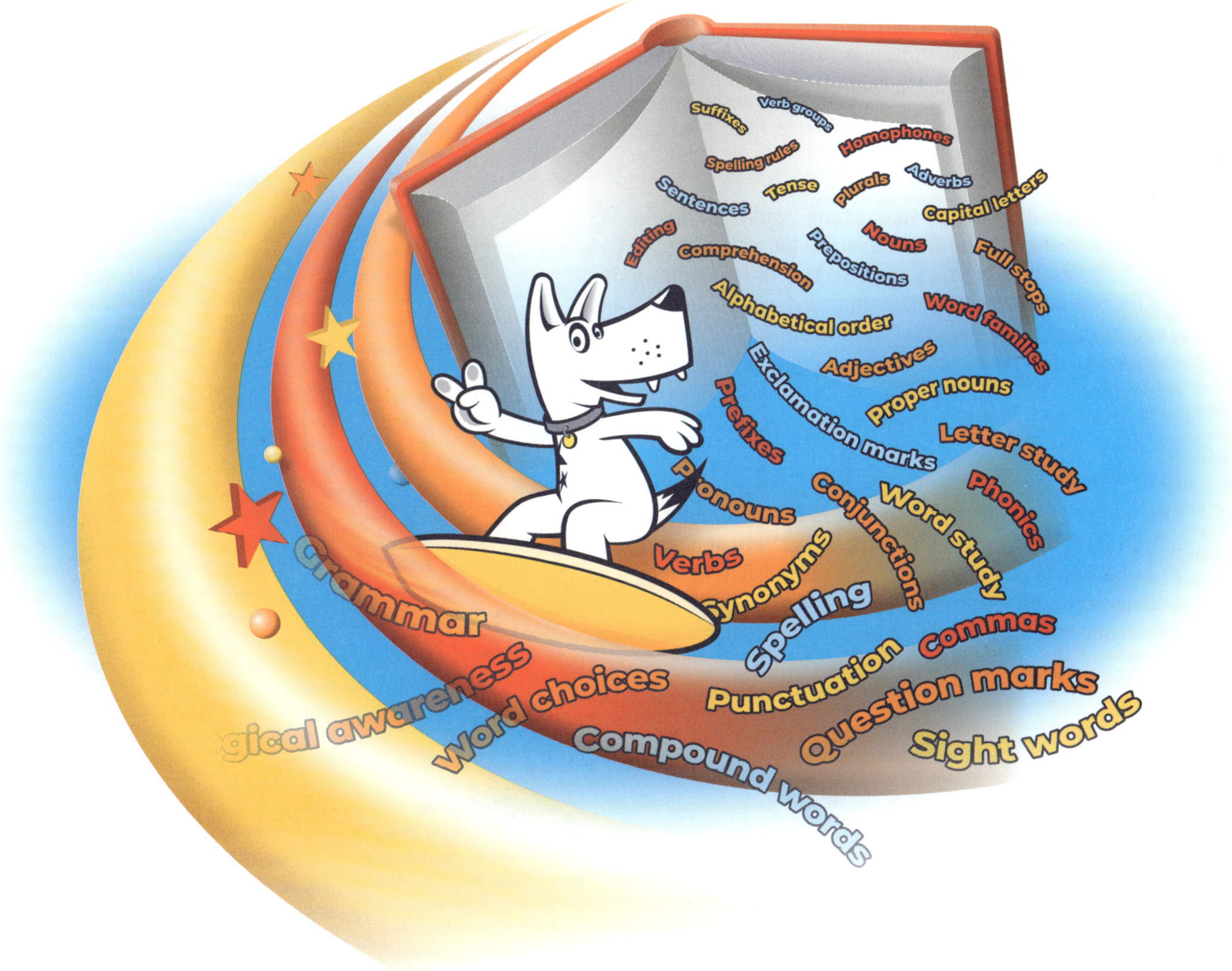

This book belongs to:

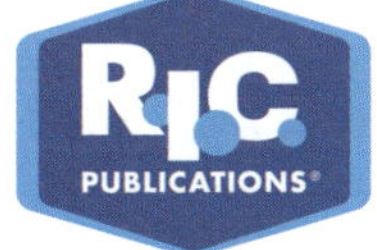

New wave English skills practice *(Book B)*

Published by R.I.C. Publications® 2014

Revised and reprinted 2022
Reprinted 2023, 2024, 2025
ISBN 978-1-922843-55-5
RIC–6221

Titles available in this series:
New wave English skills practice *(Book A)*
New wave English skills practice *(Book B)*
New wave English skills practice *(Book C)*
New wave English skills practice *(Book D)*
New wave English skills practice *(Book E)*
New wave English skills practice *(Book F)*

R.I.C. Publications® follows the guidelines for punctuation and grammar as recommended by the *Style manual for authors, editors and printers*, 2002, 6th edn.

Note, however, that teachers should use their own guide if there is a conflict.

R.I.C. Publications® acknowledges the Wadjak people of the Nyoongar Nation as the Traditional Custodians of the land on which our Western Australian office is based. We acknowledge the Traditional Custodians of Country throughout Australia and pay our respects to Elders past and present. R.I.C. Publications® recognises the role of First Nations Elders as Australia's first educators.

R.I.C. Publications®

PO Box 332
Greenwood
Western Australia 6924
+61 8 9240 9888
ricpublications.com.au
mail@ricpublications.com.au

FOREWORD

In this daily practice workbook you will be able to develop your ability to use English. Each day, you will have questions to answer in the areas of spelling, word study, punctuation and grammar. There are 160 days of questions in this workbook.

Seven weeks of each unit begin with a new skill focus. This will help remind you of some of the skills and terminology that will be used throughout the workbook. Every day, two questions will focus on the skill that is introduced at the start of the week. The remaining questions will be mixed practice which will help to improve your English skills as well as your knowledge about how language works.

At the completion of each unit, you will have the opportunity to review what you have learnt by doing one day of skill focus revision questions. Your daily scores are recorded in the bubble at the bottom of each day. These daily scores can be transferred onto the record sheets at the front of your book.

This will give an overview of your performance for the whole school year. Be sure to read each question carefully before you answer it. If you find a question too difficult, move on to the next one. If you have time at the end, you can go back to the one you haven't done.

CONTENTS

Record sheet

Week 1		Week 2		Week 3		Week 4	
Date		*Date*		*Date*		*Date*	
Skill focus		Skill focus		Skill focus		Skill focus	
Day 1		Day 1		Day 1		Day 1	
Day 2		Day 2		Day 2		Day 2	
Day 3		Day 3		Day 3		Day 3	
Day 4		Day 4		Day 4		Day 4	
Day 5		Day 5		Day 5		Day 5	

Week 5		Week 6		Week 7		Week 8	
Date		*Date*		*Date*		*Date*	
Skill focus		Skill focus		Skill focus		Day 1	
Day 1		Day 1		Day 1		Day 2	
Day 2		Day 2		Day 2		Day 3	
Day 3		Day 3		Day 3		Day 4	
Day 4		Day 4		Day 4		Day 5	
Day 5		Day 5		Day 5		Revision	

Week 9		Week 10		Week 11		Week 12	
Date		*Date*		*Date*		*Date*	
Skill focus		Skill focus		Skill focus		Skill focus	
Day 1		Day 1		Day 1		Day 1	
Day 2		Day 2		Day 2		Day 2	
Day 3		Day 3		Day 3		Day 3	
Day 4		Day 4		Day 4		Day 4	
Day 5		Day 5		Day 5		Day 5	

Week 13		Week 14		Week 15		Week 16	
Date		*Date*		*Date*		*Date*	
Skill focus		Skill focus		Skill focus		Day 1	
Day 1		Day 1		Day 1		Day 2	
Day 2		Day 2		Day 2		Day 3	
Day 3		Day 3		Day 3		Day 4	
Day 4		Day 4		Day 4		Day 5	
Day 5		Day 5		Day 5		Revision	

Record sheet

Week 17		Week 18		Week 19		Week 20	
Date		*Date*		*Date*		*Date*	
Skill focus		Skill focus		Skill focus		Skill focus	
Day 1		Day 1		Day 1		Day 1	
Day 2		Day 2		Day 2		Day 2	
Day 3		Day 3		Day 3		Day 3	
Day 4		Day 4		Day 4		Day 4	
Day 5		Day 5		Day 5		Day 5	

Week 21		Week 22		Week 23		Week 24	
Date		*Date*		*Date*		*Date*	
Skill focus		Skill focus		Skill focus		Day 1	
Day 1		Day 1		Day 1		Day 2	
Day 2		Day 2		Day 2		Day 3	
Day 3		Day 3		Day 3		Day 4	
Day 4		Day 4		Day 4		Day 5	
Day 5		Day 5		Day 5		Revision	

Week 25		Week 26		Week 27		Week 28	
Date		*Date*		*Date*		*Date*	
Skill focus		Skill focus		Skill focus		Skill focus	
Day 1		Day 1		Day 1		Day 1	
Day 2		Day 2		Day 2		Day 2	
Day 3		Day 3		Day 3		Day 3	
Day 4		Day 4		Day 4		Day 4	
Day 5		Day 5		Day 5		Day 5	

Week 29		Week 30		Week 31		Week 32	
Date		*Date*		*Date*		*Date*	
Skill focus		Skill focus		Skill focus		Day 1	
Day 1		Day 1		Day 1		Day 2	
Day 2		Day 2		Day 2		Day 3	
Day 3		Day 3		Day 3		Day 4	
Day 4		Day 4		Day 4		Day 5	
Day 5		Day 5		Day 5		Revision	

WEEK 1

Skill focus

What is a sentence?

A **sentence** is a group of words that make sense together.

They are used to share an idea.

Sentences start with a capital letter. Capital letters are big letters.

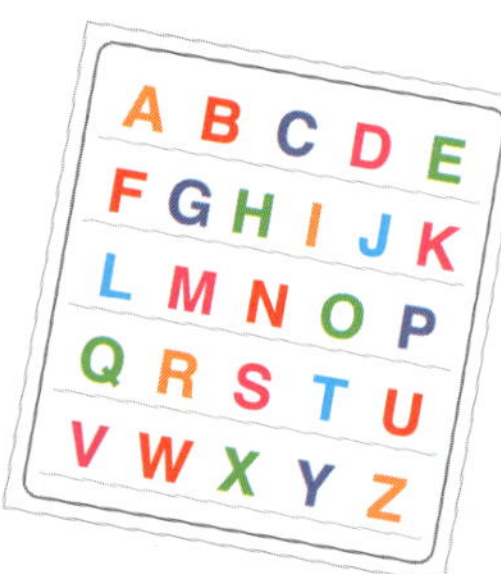

A sentence always ends with a mark to show that it is finished.

A full stop goes at the end of a 'telling' sentence.

My name is Jody.

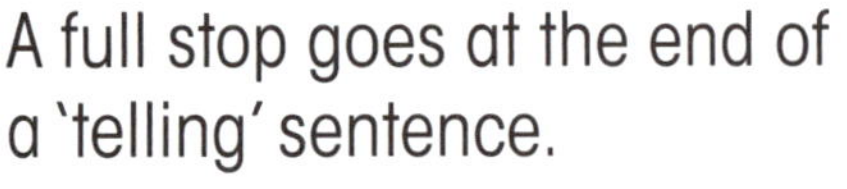

A question mark (?) goes at the end of an 'asking' sentence.

What is your name?

An exclamation mark (!) goes at the end of a 'big feeling' sentence.

I am so happy to meet you!

Practice questions

1. Add one capital letter.
   (a) there are dark clouds in the sky.
   (b) have you been on a plane?

2. Write **.** or **?** in the box.
   (a) My garden has a huge tree ☐
   (b) How old are you ☐

Day 1

1. Add one capital letter.

   my sister and I like climbing trees.

2. Write **?** or **.** in the box.

   Let's take the dog for a walk ☐

3. Correct the spelling mistake.

   We mad some cakes.

   ☐ d a m e

4. Add ***magic e*** to ***flam***.
   Hint: ***Magic e*** *goes at the end of words. It makes* ***a, e, i, o*** *and* ***u*** *say their name.*

   ☐

5. Circle the word that rhymes with ***speed***.

   spend   read   seat

6. Which word means ***shut***?

   open   close   door

7. Circle the opposite of ***last***.

   lost   fast   first

8. Write ***saw*** or ***seen***.

   The cat ☐ *the dog running.*

Day 2

1. Add one capital letter.

   do you know where I put my bag?

2. Write **!** or **?** in the box.

   When is your birthday ☐

3. Correct the spelling mistake.

   The boat is going owt to sea.

   ☐ t ou

4. Add ***magic e*** to ***crim***.

   ☐

5. Circle the word that rhymes with ***stiff***.

   cliff   lift   stick

6. Which word means ***smash***?

   brush ☐   break ☐   grab ☐

7. Circle the opposite of ***below***.

   above   bend   ground

8. Write ***saw*** or ***seen***.

   I have never ☐ *that film.*

Day 3

1. Add one capital letter.

   please may I have a drink?

2. Write **.** or **?** in the box.

   How are you today ☐

3. Correct the spelling mistake.

   I am going to buy mi lunch today.

   ☐ y m

4. Add ***magic e*** to ***plat***.

   ☐

5. Circle the word that rhymes with ***below***.

   float   grown   show

6. Which word means ***happy***?

   hop ☐   play ☐   glad ☐

7. Circle the opposite of ***never***.

   always   none   sometimes

8. Write ***to***, ***too*** or ***two***.
   Hint: ***Two*** *is a number.* ***To*** *tells us where.* ***Too*** *means also or a lot.*

   I can see ☐ *birds in the tree.*

WEEK 1

WEEK 1

Day 4

1. Add one capital letter.

   look at that horse!

2. Write **?** or **!** in the box.

   Look out ☐

3. Correct the spelling mistake.

   Our team came furst in the race.

   ☐ ir f s t

4. Add ***magic e*** to ***pin***.

   ☐

5. Circle the word that rhymes with ***food***.

   took zoo rude

6. Which word means ***hint***?

   hunt ☐ clue ☐ guess ☐

7. Circle the opposite of ***lost***.

   last found sad

8. Write ***to***, ***too*** or ***two***.

   I ate ☐ *much for dinner.*

Day 5

1. Add one capital letter.

   my best friend's name is Harriet.

2. Write **?** or **!** in the box.

   Don't touch that, it's hot ☐

3. Correct the spelling mistake.

   Mum said I cud play with you.

   ☐ oul d c

4. Add ***magic e*** to ***snak***.

   ☐

5. Circle the word that rhymes with ***made***.

   brave play spade

6. Which word means ***giggle***?

   joke ☐ laugh ☐ sing ☐

7. Circle the opposite of ***sweet***.

   strong sour tasty

8. Write ***to***, ***too*** or ***two***.

   Pavol is going ☐ *a rugby match.*

What is a noun?

Sentences are made from many different words. The words we use for people, places and things are called **nouns**.

boy

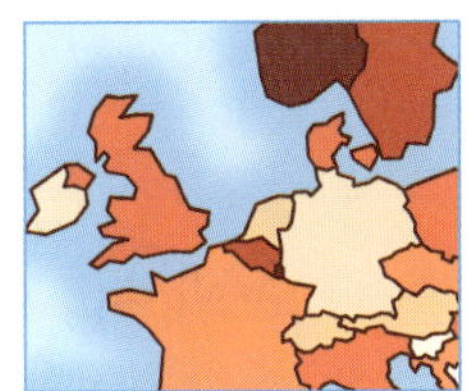
country

car

month

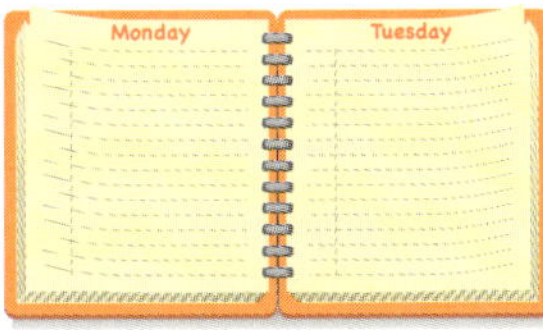

day

Nouns are naming words. Some nouns give people, places or things a special name.

Peter
Mr Brown

Australia

Toyota

Tuesday
December

Christmas

These are called proper nouns. They start with a capital letter.

Practice questions

1. Which word is the noun (naming word)?

   The tree is very tall.

   tree very tall

2. Add one capital letter.

   My name is harry.

1. Circle the noun (naming word).

   Our kitten is fluffy.

   our kitten fluffy

2. Add one capital letter.

   That book belongs to sally.

3. Correct the spelling mistake.

   We starte school at nine o'clock.

   s t t ar

4. Add ***magic e*** to ***prid***.

5. Circle the two words that rhyme.

   brown ground around

6. The word ***story*** means the same as:

   tall ☐ stung ☐ tale ☐

7. Write **.** or **!** in the box.

   Help me ☐

8. Write ***for*** or ***four***.

   I like to take the dog ☐ *a walk.*

Day 2

1. Circle the noun (naming word).

   I like playing football.

   like playing football

2. Add two capital letters.

   My teacher's name is mrs jones.

3. Correct the spelling mistake.

   They wer late for school.

   [ ] ere w

4. Add ***magic e*** to ***ston***.

   [ ]

5. The word [ ] rhymes with ***ball***.

   balloon [ ] talk [ ] crawl [ ]

6. Circle the opposite of ***awake***.

   around asleep snore

7. Add two capital letters.

   he lived in scotland.

8. Write ***buy*** or ***by***.

   We come to school [ ] *bus.*

Day 3

1. Circle the noun (naming word).

   The little girl was crying.

2. Add two capital letters.

   is your birthday in april?

3. Correct the spelling mistake.

   He shud have worn a coat.

   [ ] oul sh d

4. Add ***magic e*** to ***slid***.

   [ ]

5. Circle the two words that rhyme.

   now blow grow

6. The word ***hurt*** means the same as:

   help [ ] harm [ ] harp [ ]

7. Write ***?*** or ***!*** in the box.

   Is that coat warm [ ]

8. Write ***for*** or ***four***.

   There are [ ] *slices left.*

Day 4

1. Circle the noun (naming word).

   Where did you put your shoes?

2. Add two capital letters.

   My dentist is called mr bishop.

3. Correct the spelling mistake.

   I <u>liv</u> in the same street as my friend.

4. Add ***magic e*** to ***glob***.

5. The word ______ rhymes with ***hear***.

   pear ☐ bear ☐ year ☐

6. Circle the opposite of ***brave***.

   hard strong afraid

7. Add two capital letters.

   have you been to germany?

8. Write ***buy*** or ***by***.

   We are going to ______ our lunch.

Day 5

1. Circle the noun (naming word).

   We camped near the river.

2. Add two capital letters.

   olivia was away on tuesday.

3. Correct the spelling mistake.

   I wish I could have <u>sum</u> more.

   me o s

4. Add ***magic e*** to ***smil***.

5. Circle the two words that rhyme.

   train said lane

6. The word ***stone*** means the same as:

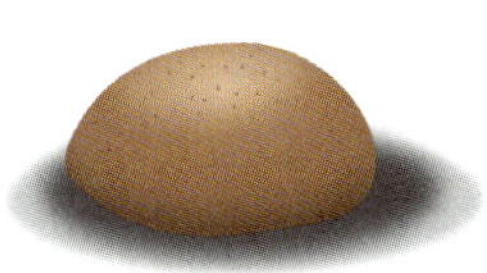

   hard ☐ rock ☐ stick ☐

7. Write **.** or **!** in the box.

   My brother is older than Ben ☐

8. Finish the sentence with ***me*** or ***my***.

   My uncle sent ______ a present.

WEEK 2

Skill focus

More than one person, place or thing

How can we show that we have more than one of something?

We usually add ***s*** to the end of the words.

two bikes *three birds* *four beans*

five stars *six books*

For some words that end with ***s***, ***x***, ***z***, ***ch*** and ***sh*** we add ***es*** instead.

two buses *three foxes* *four buzzes*

five peaches *six wishes*

The word we use for more than one person or thing is called a **plural**.

Practice questions

1. Add ***s*** or ***es*** to make the word plural.

   One box, three ______

   One cat, three ______

2. Write the plural of ***book***.

Day 1

1. Write the plural of ***rock***.

   one rock, two ______

2. Add ***s*** or ***es*** to make the word plural.

   dish______

3. Correct the spelling mistake.

   Please water the plants in eech pot.

   ______ ch ea

4. Add ***magic e*** to ***flut***.

   ______

5. Circle the word that does NOT rhyme with ***paid***.

   made laid pay

6. Circle the opposite of ***rich***.

   spent cost poor

7. Add two capital letters.
   *Hint: The word **I** is always a capital letter.*

   danny and i sit next to each other.

8. Which word is a noun (naming word)?

   ship big

Day 2

1. Write the plural of ***dog***.

   one dog, two ☐

2. Add ***s*** or ***es*** to make the word plural.

   dress☐

3. Correct the spelling mistake.

   I <u>fownd</u> a shell on the beach.

   ☐ n d ou f

4. Add ***magic e*** to ***spok***.

   ☐

5. Write ***of*** or ***off***.
   Hint: off is the opposite of on.

   Be careful not to fall ☐ *your bike.*

6. Write ***be*** or ***bee***.

   I will ☐ *there at two o'clock.*

7. Add two capital letters.

   can you meet me on monday?

8. Which word is a noun (naming word)?

   funny   clown

MY SCORE

Day 3

1. Write the plural of ***shop***.

   one shop, two ☐

2. Add ***s*** or ***es*** to make the word plural.

   lunch☐

3. Correct the spelling mistake.

   I'll wait here <u>wile</u> you are in the shop.

   wh l i e

4. Add ***magic e*** to ***cut***.

   ☐

5. Circle the word that does NOT rhyme with ***foil***.

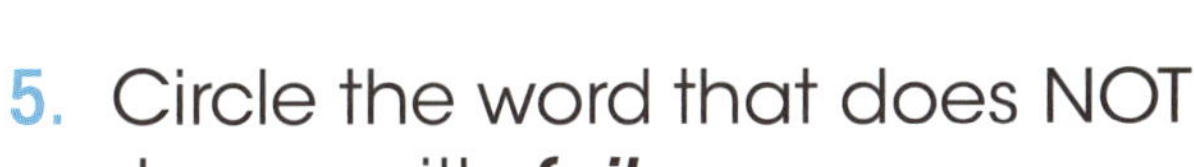

   coin   soil   oil

6. The word ***coat*** means the same as:

   boat ☐   scarf ☐   jacket ☐

7. Add two capital letters.

   Dad and i have birthdays in march.

8. Circle the two nouns (naming words) in this sentence.

   The dog chased the cat.

MY SCORE

Day 4

1. Write the plural of ***bag***.

   one bag, two ☐

2. Add ***s*** or ***es*** to make the word plural.

   brush☐

3. Correct the spelling mistake.

   A lion and a cheetah run very <u>farst</u>.

   ☐ f s a t

4. Add ***magic e*** to ***phon***.

5. Write ***of*** or ***off***.

   Which one ☐ *you made this mess?*

6. Write ***be*** or ***bee***.

   A

   can make honey.

7. Add two capital letters.

   the concert is next wednesday.

8. Circle the two nouns (naming words) in this sentence.

   The spade is in the shed.

Day 5

1. Write the plural of ***bike***.

   one bike, two ☐

2. Add ***s*** or ***es*** to make the word plural.

   tax☐

3. Correct the spelling mistake.

   We walk to <u>scool</u> every day.

   ☐

4. Add ***magic e*** to ***hug***.

5. Circle the word that does NOT rhyme with ***new***.

   who　　true　　so

6. The word ☐ is the opposite of ***there***.

   here　　then　　away

7. Add two capital letters.

   ben and i like computer games.

8. Circle the two nouns (naming words) in this sentence.

   I have a sister and a brother.

What is a verb?

Sentences are made from many different words. Words that tell us what someone or something is doing are called **verbs**.

run

jump

sleep

yell

Verbs are action words. Every sentence needs a verb (action word).

Sometimes we add ***-ed*** or ***-ing*** to the end of verbs (action words).

When we add ***-ed*** to a verb (action word), it tells us that it has already happened.

When we add ***-ing*** to a verb (action word), it tells us that it is happening now.

	Already happened	Happening now

cook	*Mum cook<u>ed</u> dinner.*	*Look at her cook<u>ing</u>.*

Practice questions

1. Which word is the verb (doing word)?

   She ran across the path.

   She   ran   path

2. Add ***ed*** or ***ing***.

   (a) The pot is boil [ ] over.

   (b) The plane has land [ ] on time.

---

1. Which word is the doing word (verb)?

   The lion roared loudly.

   lion   roared   loudly

2. Add ***ed*** or ***ing***.

   She reach [ ] up to turn it off.

3. Correct the spelling mistake.

   We <u>lik</u> fish and chips.

   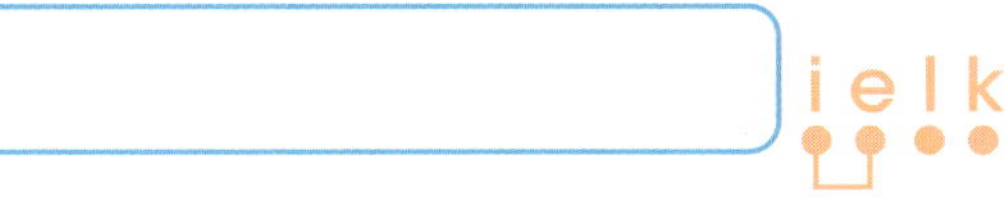

4. Write the missing letters. ***nk*** or ***gk***

   I thi [ ] it's going to rain soon.

5. Add ***s*** or ***es*** to make the word plural.

   chick [ ]

6. Which word? ***of*** or ***off***

   One [ ] them will get it for you.

7. Write **.** or **?** in the box.

   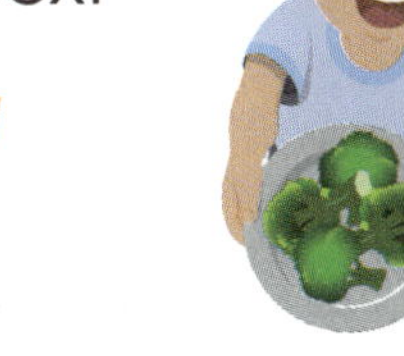

   Do you like eating broccoli [ ]

8. Circle the noun that needs a capital letter.

   I like long walks in october.

Day 2

1. Which word is the verb (doing word)?

   The breeze blew gently.

   breeze   blew   gently

2. Add ***ed*** or ***ing***.

   We are help____ to rake the leaves.

3. Correct the spelling mistake.

   We go shopping every Thusday.

   ay d Th ur s

4. Add ***magic e*** to ***prun***.

5. Add ***s*** or ***es*** to make the word plural.

   bench____

6. Circle the word that means ***start***.

   stop   doing   begin

7. Add two capital letters.

   my sister and i are twins.

8. Circle the two nouns in this sentence.

   We get wool from sheep.

Day 3

1. Which word is the verb (doing word)?

   The baby cries a lot.

2. Add ***ed*** or ***ing***.

   My gran is rest____ in the chair.

3. Correct the spelling mistake.

   Mum picked the pritty flowers.

   r e tt p y

4. Write the missing letters. ***ve*** or ***fe***

   The opposite of afraid is bra____.

5. Add ***s*** or ***es*** to make the word plural.

   tree____

6. Which word? ***of*** or ***off***

   Jamie is one ____ my best friends.

7. Write ***!*** or ***?*** in the box.

   I hate broccoli____

8. Circle the two nouns that need capital letters.

   Valera and Ben are going to africa and australia.

Day 4

1. Which word is the verb (doing word)?

   I packed my books away.

2. Add ***ed*** or ***ing***.

   Mum paint[ ] the kitchen on Sunday.

3. Correct the spelling mistake.

   We go to church every Sonday.

   [ ] ay d S n u

4. Add ***magic e*** to ***rud***.

   [ ]

5. Add ***s*** or ***es*** to make the word plural.

   wish[ ]

6. Circle the opposite of ***under***.

   higher   over   down

7. Add capital letters to two words.

   Mum said i could go in june.

8. Circle the two nouns in this sentence.

   My favourite fruit is the banana.

Day 5

1. Circle the verb (doing word).

   The girl is walking the dog.

2. Add ***ed*** or ***ing***.

   Dad told me not to wake the sleep[ ] baby.

3. Correct the spelling mistake.

   I like to run arownd the playground.

   [ ] n d a r ou

4. Write the missing letters. ***ie*** or ***ei***

   Her best fr[ ]nd lives next door.

5. Add ***s*** or ***es*** to make the word plural.

   cup[ ]

6. Which word? ***of*** or ***off***

   Can you please get  *my bag?*

7. Write **.** or **?** in the box.

   I am going to eat green beans instead[ ]

8. Circle the noun that needs a capital letter.

   My friend lives in italy.

WEEK 4

Skill focus

Compound words

Some words can be joined to make new words. These are called **compound words**.

rain + bow = rainbow

hand + bag = handbag

tooth + brush = toothbrush

Compound words do not have the same meaning as the two words that they are made from.

Practice questions

1. Choose two words to make a compound word.

   (a) book cook bow

   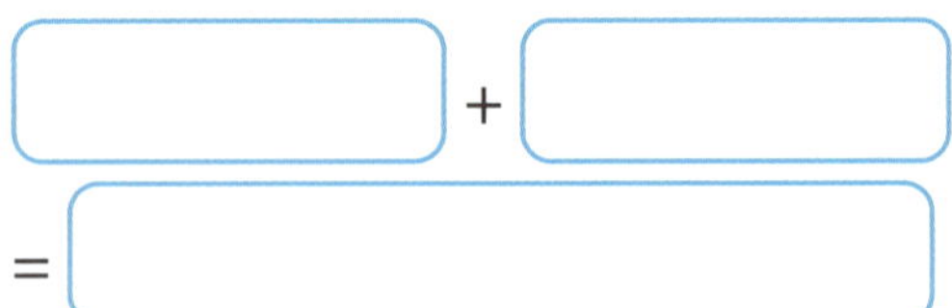

   (b) ball hot foot

   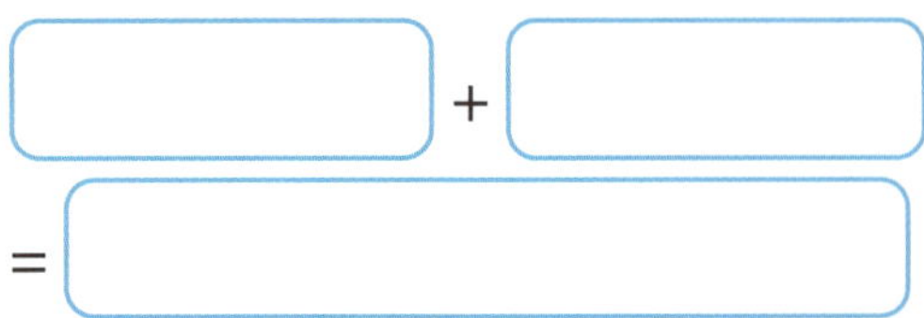

2. Put a circle around each word that makes ***playground***.

   playground

Day 1

1. Choose two words to make a compound word.

   butter book fly

   \+ =

2. Put a circle around each word that makes ***raincoat***.

   raincoat

3. Correct the spelling mistake.

   Don't forget to brin your hat.

   ng i b r

4. Write the plural of ***puzzle***.

5. Add ***ed*** or ***ing***.

   My sister and I like play hopscotch.

6. The word ***never*** means:

   sometimes not ever always

7. Add two capital letters.

   You and i will go on friday.

8. Circle the verb (doing word).

   The girl jumped into the swimming pool.

Day 2

1. Choose two words to make a compound word.

   ball foot door

   ☐ + ☐ =

   ☐

2. Put a circle around each word that makes ***butterfly***.

   butterfly

3. Correct the spelling mistake.

   My teacher gave me a reward for doing grate work.

   ☐ ea g r t

4. Add ***oa*** and ***ow***.

   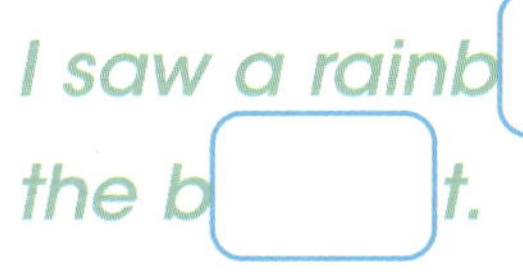

   I saw a rainb☐ over the b☐t.

5. 

   two horses, one

   ☐

6. Write ***sea*** or ***see***.

   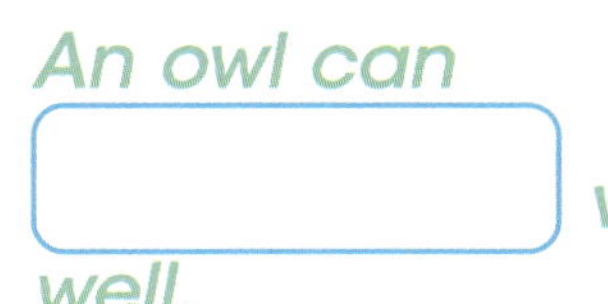

   An owl can ☐ very well.

7. Add two capital letters.

   jess and jake sit next to each other.

8. Circle the verb (doing word).

   Ben eats apples and bananas.

MY SCORE

Day 3

1. Choose two words to make a compound word.

   play yard farm

   ☐ + ☐ =

   ☐

2. Put a circle around each word that makes ***sunshine***.

   sunshine

3. Correct the spelling mistake.

   I play football on Sataday.

   ☐ d ay ur S a t

4. Write the plural of ***peach***.

5. Add ***ed*** or ***ing***.

   I walk☐ to school this morning.

6. Circle the opposite of ***below***.

   blow above ground

7. Add two capital letters.

   our cat's name is fluffy.

8. Circle the verb (doing word).

   The dog chewed a bone.

MY SCORE

WEEK 5

WEEK 5

Day 4

1. Choose two words to make a compound word.

sun round set

_____ + _____ =

2. Put a circle around each word that makes ***farmyard***.

farmyard

3. Correct the spelling mistake.

The little gurl lost her doll.

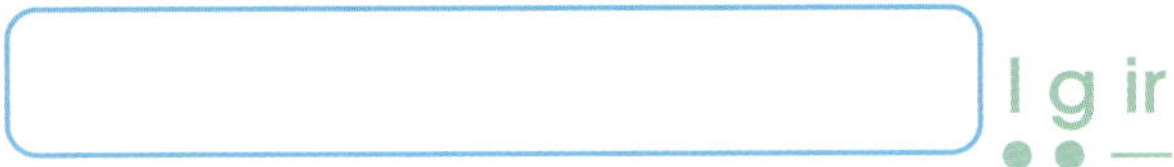

l g ir

4. Add ***oa*** and ***ow***.

The sparr___ flew over the c___st.

5. two buses, one

6. Write ***sea*** or ***see***.

Fish swim in the _____.

7. Add two capital letters.

we buy our lunch on thursdays.

8. Circle the verbs (doing words).

The mouse ran and Mum screamed.

MY SCORE

Day 5

1. Choose two words to make a compound word.

play fun ground

_____ + _____ =

2. Put a circle around each word that makes ***sunset***.

sunset

3. Correct the spelling mistake.

I fownd my shoe in the toy box.

ou n f d

4. Write the plural of ***teacher***.

5. Add ***ed*** or ***ing***.

Dad cook___ a tasty breakfast for us.

6. The word ***harm*** means:

hurt make better heat

7. Add two capital letters.

Her name is sophie townsend.

8. Circle the verbs (doing words).

She laughed so much that she cried!

MY SCORE

What is an adjective?

Sentences are made from many different words. Words that describe something or someone are called **adjectives**.

*The **tall** man is playing basketball.*

*The **pretty** flowers are growing in the garden.*

Adjectives (describing words) sometimes come after the person or thing they are describing.

*The bird's feathers are **soft**.*

*Dad's shirt is **red**.*

Practice questions

1. Which word is the adjective that describes the jacket?

   The teacher is wearing a red jacket.

   teacher   wearing   red

2. Which word is the adjective that describes the tail?

   The dog's tail is long.

   dog   tail   long

---

1. Which word is the adjective that describes the hair?

   Do you have curly hair?

   you   curly   hair

2. Circle the better describing word.

   The angry/fluffy lion roared loudly.

3. Correct the spelling mistake.

   It stings when soap gets in yor eyes.

   [ ] our y

4. Add ***ai*** or ***ay***.

   I think it could r[ ]n later.

5. Write a compound word starting with ***rain***.

   bow   time   wet

   [ ]

6. Add ***did*** or ***done***.

   Isabel [ ] her best work today.

7. Write **.** or **?** in the box.

   Have you had a ride on a camel[ ]

8. Write the correct verb (doing word): ***chase*** or ***chased***.

   The small dog [ ] the large cat.

Day 2

1. Which word is the adjective that describes the car?

   The black car is over there.

   black car there

2. Circle the better describing word.

   Kim felt happy when she got a new/bored toy.

3. Correct the spelling mistake.

   I want to plaiy a game.

   l p ay

4. Write **stop**, **stopped** or **stopping**.

   He ______ what he was doing.

5. Add **ed** or **ing**.

   I fill  *up my drink bottle.*

6. Circle the two words that rhyme.

   about loud shout

7. Add two capital letters.

   We are going to england in august.

8. Circle the verb (doing word).

   We moved house a few weeks ago.

Day 3

1. Which word is the adjective that describes the bike?

   Jimmy's bike is fast.

2. Circle the better describing word.

   I like playing in my gentle/clean room.

3. Correct the spelling mistake.

   I have my oan room.

   n ow

4. Add **ai** or **ay**.

   This ch____r is very comfortable.

5. Write a compound word ending with **fish**.

   small gold fin

6. Add **did** or **done**.

   What have you  *?*

7. Write **.** or **?** in the box.

   I'm going to play with my cat ____

8. Write the correct verb (doing word): **drop** or **dropped**.

   If you ______ the glass, it will break.

Day 4

1. Which word is the adjective that describes the water?

   The water at the beach was cold.

2. Circle the better describing word.

   The shiny/gentle dog sniffed the baby.

3. Correct the spelling mistake.

   Thay are riding their bikes.

   [ ] ey Th

4. Write **help**, **helped** or **helping**.

   We like to [ ] *to feed our cat.*

5. Add **ed** or **ing**.

   Our time on the playground has end[ ].

6. Circle the two words that rhyme.

   lie cry dried

7. Add two capital letters.

   can James and i play outside?

8. Circle the verb (doing word).

   Dad and I fished on the river.

Day 5

1. Which word is the adjective that describes the elephant's trunk?

   The elephant has a long trunk.

2. Circle the better describing word.

   The kind/long lady smiled at me.

3. Correct the spelling mistake.

   Woud you like another slice?

   [ ] oul W d

4. Add **ai** or **ay**.

   I hear the tr[ ]*n coming.*

5. Write a compound word starting with **sun**.

   cloud rain flower

   [ ]

6. Add **did** or **done**.

   I have [ ] *all my homework.*

7. Write **.** or **!** in the box.

   The wind blew the leaves[ ]

8. Write the correct verb (doing word): **talk** or **talked**.

   The lady [ ] *loudly on the phone.*

Skill focus

Comparing two or more things

Adjectives (describing words) are used to tell us more about the person, place or thing in a sentence.

If we want to compare two or more people or things, we add ***er*** or ***est*** to the describing word.

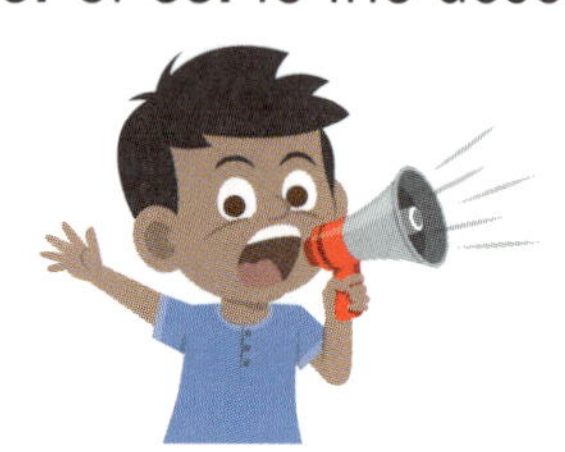

loud

*The boy is **loud**.*

louder

*The girl is **louder**.*

loudest

*The dog is the **loudest**.*

Practice questions

1. Write ***tall***, ***taller*** or ***tallest***.

   The tree is ____ *than the ladder.*

2. Write ***small***, ***smaller*** or ***smallest***.

   Which is the ____, *a car, a bicycle or a train?*

3. Add ***er*** and ***est*** to ***strong***.

   strong + er = ____

   strong + est = ____

Day 1

1. Add ***er*** to ***small***.

   small + er = ____

2. Write ***fresh***, ***fresher*** or ***freshest***.

   Dad bought the ____ *eggs from the farmer.*

3. Correct the spelling mistake.

   How olld is your dad?

   ____ d o l

4. two sandwiches, one

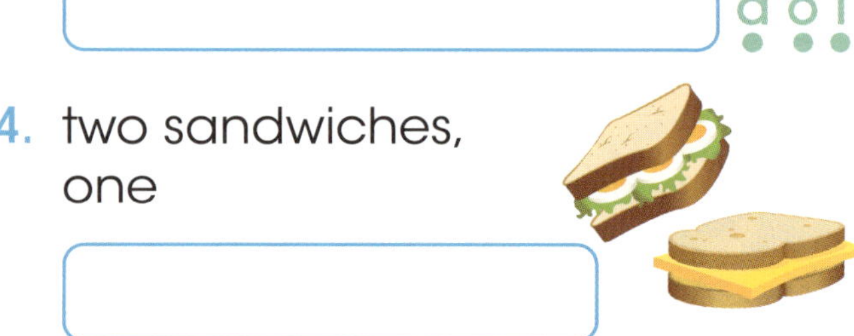

   ____

5. Write a compound word ending with ***paper***.

   dirty news brown

   ____

6. Circle the opposite of ***mean***.

   happy kind tired

7. Write **.** or ***!*** in the box.

   Watch out ____

8. Which word is the adjective that describes the ***kitten***?

   The cute kitten was curled up asleep.

   cute kitten asleep

Day 2

1. Add ***er*** to ***fresh***.

   fresh + er = ☐

2. Write ***quick***, ***quicker*** or ***quickest***.

   A beetle is ☐ *than a snail.*

3. Correct the spelling mistake.

   Munday comes after Sunday.

   ☐ ay M o n d

4. Pick ***ai***, ***ay***, ***oa*** or ***ow***.

   The black piece of c☐l will st☐n my hands.

5. Write ***flour*** or ***flower***.

   The cake needed two cups of ☐.

6. Circle the word that means ***story***.

   tail tale

7. Circle the noun that needs a capital letter.

   rabbit july soft

8. Which word is the adjective that describes the ***rabbit***?

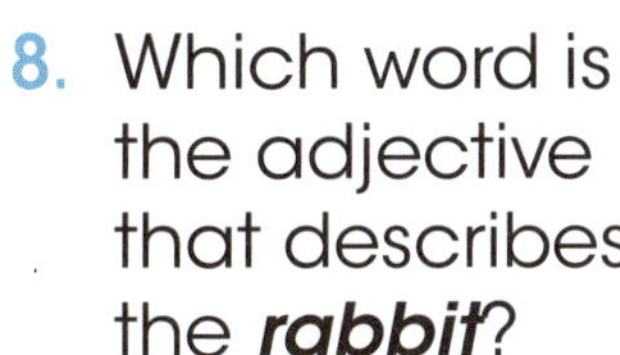

   The furry rabbit hopped on the grass.

   grass furry hopped

Day 3

1. Add ***est*** to ***quick***.

   quick + est = ☐

2. Write ***pretty***, ***prettier*** or ***prettiest***.

   This flower is ☐ *than that flower.*

3. Correct the spelling mistake.

   He arrived at school arfter the bell.

   ☐ er a f t

4. five ants, one ☐

5. Add a word to make a compound word.

   class☐

   new room shoe

6. Circle the word that means ***spot***.

   line dot spoon

7. Write **.** or **?** in the box.

   When will we get there☐

8. Circle the adjective that describes the ***pencil***.

   This is the sharpest pencil.

Day 4

1. Add **est** to **tall**.

   tall + est = ☐

2. Write **heavy**, **heavier** or **heaviest**.

   That ☐ book is on the shelf.

3. Correct the spelling mistake.

   We are having a test on Wenesday.

   ☐ W e dne ay s d

4. Pick **ai**, **ay**, **oa** or **ow**.

   On holid☐, I sailed on a yell☐ b☐t.

5. Write **flour** or **flower**.

   A bee landed on the ☐.

6. Write **tale** or **tail**.

   A fox has a bushy ☐.

7. Circle the noun that does NOT need a capital letter.

   august　　january　　week

8. Circle the adjective that describes the **gate**.

   Dad will fix the rusty gate.

MY SCORE

Day 5

1. Add **est** to **cold**.

   cold + est = ☐

2. Write **cold**, **colder** or **coldest**.

   Today is ☐ than yesterday.

3. Correct the spelling mistake.

   I like Fridays beekos we don't get homework.

   ☐ c b e au se

4. three foxes, one

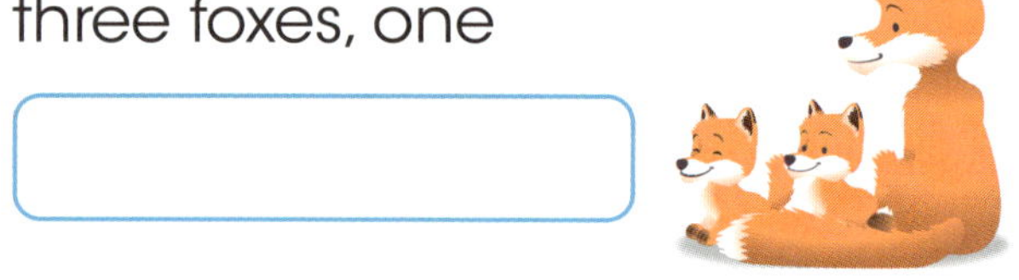

5. Write a compound word starting with **air**.

   air☐

   bird　　fly　　port

6. Circle the opposite of **live**.

   love　　give　　die

7. Write **.** or **!** in the box.

   I'll empty the dishwasher☐

8. Circle the adjective that describes the **hill**.

   We climbed up the steep hill.

MY SCORE

WEEK 8

Day 1

1. Correct the spelling mistake.

   The balloon floated off intoo the sky.

   n i t o

2. Write the missing letters. ***us*** or ***uss***

   We catch the b____ to school.

3. Write ***of*** or ***have***.
   Hint: Use ***have*** *(not* ***of****) after the words* ***should, could*** *or* ***would****.*

   We should ____ left earlier for school.

4. Circle the opposite of ***best***.

   good worst test

5. Write the plural of ***branch***.

6. Add two capital letters.

   We are going to france in august.

7. Circle the adjective (describing word).

   A watermelon is green on the outside.

8. Add ***er*** or ***est*** to the adjective (describing word).

   My brother is old____ than Jill.

Day 2

1. Correct the spelling mistake.

   I forgot to aks my mum to wash my jumper.

   k a s

2. Write the missing letters. ***sk*** or ***sc***

   I have freckles on my ____in.

3. Write ***here*** or ***hear***.

   We could not ____ her singing.

4. Circle the word that means the same as ***over***.

   above high down

5. Circle the two words that rhyme.

   hang sing sang

6. Write ***?*** or ***!*** in the box.

   Can you count to one million

7. Is ***fish*** a noun or a verb?

   Look at the fish in the tank.

   noun verb

8. Add ***er*** or ***est*** to the adjective (describing word).

   Kate has the long____ hair in the class.

WEEK 8

Day 3

1. Correct the spelling mistake.

   The class has gorn to the library.

   [ ] o ne g

2. Write the missing letter(s). ***z*** or ***zz***

   A bee can bu[ ] and sting.

3. Write ***of*** or ***have***.

   The class could [ ] been better at lining up.

4. Circle the opposite of ***take***.

   get give drop

5. Write the plural of ***key***.

   [ ]

6. Add two capital letters.

   the month of may has 31 days.

7. Circle the adjective (describing word).

   The smelly socks are being cleaned.

8. Add ***er*** or ***est*** to the adjective (describing word).

   Wool is soft[ ] than wood.

Day 4

1. Correct the spelling mistake.

   Fryday is the day before Saturday.

   [ ] d ay F r i

2. Write the missing letters. ***sh*** or ***ch***

   The ri[ ] lady had lots of money.

3. Write ***here*** or ***hear***.

   We are waiting over [ ].

4. Circle the word that means the same as ***big***.

   tiny heavy large

5. Circle the two words that rhyme.

   plant stand ant

6. Write **.** or **?** in the box.

   A beetle is an insect[ ]

7. Is ***elephant*** a noun or a verb?

   Have you ever seen an elephant?

   noun verb

8. Add ***er*** or ***est*** to the adjective (describing word).

   I am the young[ ] in my family.

Day 5

1. Correct the spelling mistake.

   Do you want to come to my house on Toosday?

   [ ] ue s T ay d

2. Write the missing letters. ***sc*** or ***sk***

   Your brain is in your [ ] ull.

3. Write ***of*** or ***have***.

   We would [ ] gone with you.

4. Circle the opposite of ***low***.

   high up tall

5. Write the plural of ***six***.

   [ ]

6. Add two capital letters.

   Gran and i went shopping on saturday.

7. Circle the describing word (adjective).

   Laura's football is blue.

8. Add ***er*** or ***est*** to the adjective.

   Dad is the tall [ ] in our family.

Skill focus review

WEEK 8

1. Correct the spelling mistake.

   Do you know yor address?

   [ ] our y

2. Add ***es*** or ***s*** to make a plural.

   beach [ ]

3. Choose two words to make a compound word.

   house light yellow

   [ ] + [ ] =

   [ ]

4. Write ***!*** or ***?*** in the box.

   Stop kicking that wall right now [ ]

5. Circle the noun (naming word) that needs a capital letter.

   month april day

6. Circle the verb (doing word).

   I packed my bag for school.

7. Circle the adjective (describing word).

   Dad washed the dirty dishes.

8. Add ***er*** or ***est*** to the adjective.

   What is the fast [ ] you can run?

Skill focus

Different types of sentences

A **sentence** is a group of words that make sense together.

They start with a capital letter and have a mark to show where they end.

There are different types of sentences. They tell us what type of mark to use at the end.

Use a full stop when the sentence is telling you about something. •

Cara is my best friend.

Use a full stop when the sentence is telling you to do something. •

Put your lunch box in your bag.

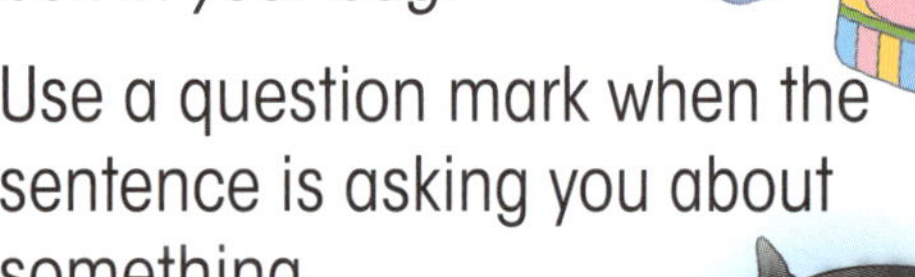

Use a question mark when the sentence is asking you about something. ?

Where is the cat?

Use an exclamation mark when the sentence shows a strong feeling. !

Watch out for that step!

Practice questions

1. Write **.**, **!** or **?** in the box.
   (a) I love hearing funny jokes ☐
   (b) Do you have freckles ☐
   (c) Look out ☐

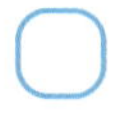

2. When can we go home? This sentence is:
   telling something. ☐
   asking something. ☐
   showing a strong feeling. ☐

Day 1

1. Write **?** or **!** in the box.
   Can you see the snail on the plant ☐

2. The sentence above is:
   asking something. ☐
   showing a strong feeling. ☐

3. Correct the spelling mistake.
   My cousin <u>caim</u> over on Saturday.
   ☐ a e m c

4. Add ***ed*** or ***ing***.
   The bird was fly☐ high in the sky.

5. Circle the opposite of ***easy***.
   work   hard   please

6. Add two capital letters.
   the twins were born on 25 june.

7. Circle the two nouns.
   She put the cake in the oven.

8. Are the underlined words nouns or verbs?
   The huge lion <u>climbed</u> to the top of the rock and <u>roared</u>.
   nouns   verbs

WEEK 9

Day 2

1. Write **?** or **!** in the box.

   What a surprise ☐

2. The sentence above is:

   asking something. ☐

   showing a strong feeling. ☐

3. Add ***ee*** and sound out each word.

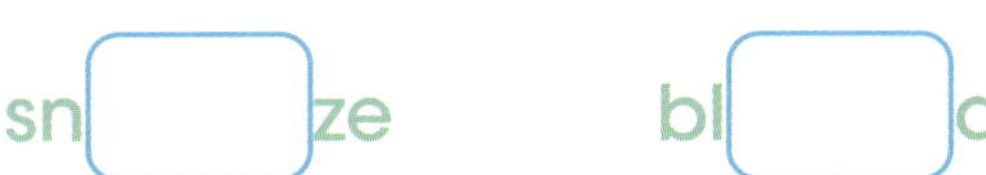

   sn☐ze   bl☐d

4. Circle the word rhyming with ***shows***.

   nose   sound   how

5. The word means the same as ***wet***.

   damp   muddy   cold

6. Add two capital letters.

   may Laura and i draw some pictures?

7. Which word is NOT a noun?

   We have two birds and a rabbit.

   birds   and   rabbit

8. Circle the verb.

   You know the words of the song.

MY SCORE

Day 3

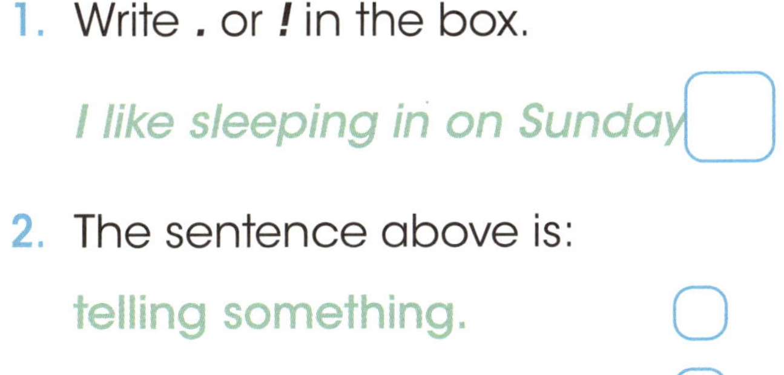

1. Write **.** or **!** in the box.

   I like sleeping in on Sunday ☐

2. The sentence above is:

   telling something. ☐

   showing a strong feeling. ☐

3. Correct the spelling mistake.

   We will tri to visit Uncle David on Sunday.

   ☐ y t r

4. Add ***ed*** or ***ing***.

   The dog yawn☐ and stretched.

5. Circle the word that means the same as ***enormous***.

   little   huge   empty

6. Add two capital letters.

   on sunday, we walked along the river.

7. Circle the two nouns.

   The sand on the beach was hot.

8. Are the underlined words nouns or verbs?

   Dad parked the car in the garage and locked the door.

   nouns   verbs

MY SCORE

Day 4

1. Write **?** or **!** in the box.

   Have you camped in a tent ☐

2. The sentence above is:

   asking something. ☐

   showing a strong feeling. ☐

3. Add ***ee*** and sound out each word.

   sw☐t betw☐n

4. Circle the word rhyming with ***bird***.

   turn word hurt

5. Circle the opposite of ***dark***.

   light black down

6. Add two capital letters.

   halloween is the last day of october.

7. Which word is NOT a noun?

   The silly clown rode the tiny bike.

   silly clown bike

8. Circle the verb.

   I asked my mum and dad for a new scooter.

Day 5

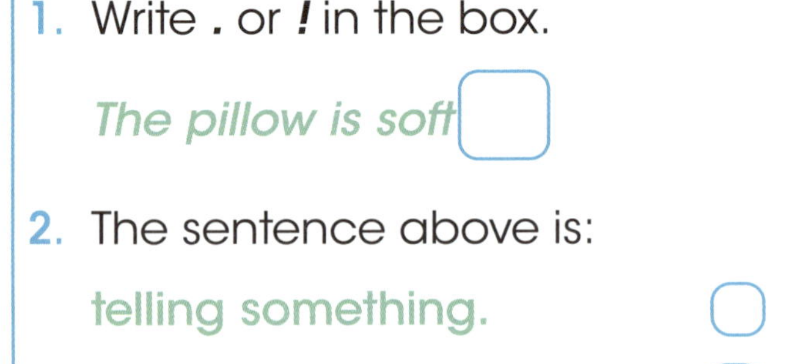

1. Write **.** or **!** in the box.

   The pillow is soft ☐

2. The sentence above is:

   telling something. ☐

   showing a strong feeling. ☐

3. Correct the spelling mistake.

   Our kite got caught in the trea.

   ☐ ee t r

4. Add ***ed*** or ***ing***.

   It was rain☐ *a lot during the week.*

5. Which word means the same as ***quick***?

   run slow fast

6. Add two capital letters.

   our family is going to japan soon.

7. Circle the two nouns.

   Can you see the snail on the leaf?

8. Are the underlined words nouns or verbs?

   My cousin baked a cake and shared it with us.

   nouns verbs

Skill focus

Alphabetical order

The letters in our alphabet have an order.

a b c d e f g h i j k l m n o p q r s t u v w x y z

This is called **alphabetical order**. Alphabetical order always stays the same.

We can put words in alphabetical order too.

To put words in alphabetical order, look at the first letter of each word:

zebra monkey ant star

The word starting with the letter that comes first in the alphabet goes first. The word ***ant*** starts with ***a*** so it is the first word.

a b c d e f g h i j k l m n o p q r s t u v w x y z

a n t

The next word is the one whose first letter is next in the alphabet.

a b c d e f g h i j k l m n o p q r s t u v w x y z

ant monkey

Keep going until all your words are in alphabetical order.

a b c d e f g h i j k l m n o p q r s t u v w x y z

ant monkey star zebra

Practice questions

1. The word ______ comes first in alphabetical order.

   drum bone skip

2. The word ______ comes second in alphabetical order.

   snake camel mouse

Day 1

WEEK 10

1. Add the missing letter.

   a b c  e

2. Circle the word that comes first in alphabetical order.

   bird ant crow

3. Correct the spelling mistake.

   We had 15 minutes more to wate.

   ______ ai t w

4. two pinches, one ______

5. Write ***blue*** or ***blew***.

   The wind ______ the fence over.

6. Write ***!*** or ***?*** in the box.

   Can you touch your toes ☐

7. Circle the word that is the adjective.

   The teacher told us a funny joke.

   funny told joke

8. Write ***longer*** or ***longest***.

   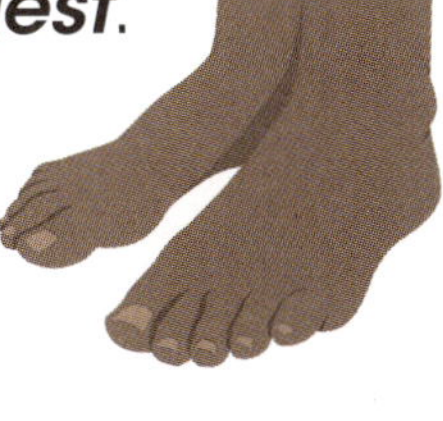

   One of my feet is ______ than the other.

a b c d e f g h i j k l m
n o p q r s t u v w x y z

WEEK 10

Day 2

1. Add the missing letter.

f g [ ] i j k

2. Circle the word that comes first in alphabetical order.

white yellow red

3. Add *ea* and sound out each word.

t[ ]m l[ ]f

4. Circle the two rhyming words.

born for worn

5. Write *am* or *is*.

It [ ] a sunny day.

6. Write *.* or *?* in the box.

Will it rain today[ ]

7. Circle the adjective that describes the *clown*.

The silly clown fell over.

8. Add *er* or *est* to the adjective.

My pencil is long[ ] than my ruler.

a b c d e f g h i j k l m
n o p q r s t u v w x y z

MY SCORE

Day 3

1. Add the missing letter.

l m n o [ ]

2. Circle the word that comes first in alphabetical order.

sheep ant goat

3. Correct the spelling mistake.

I onlee have one chocolate left.

[ ] l y o n

4. Write the plural of *switch*.

[ ]

5. Write *sail* or *sale*.

Those toys are in the [ ].

6. Write *.* or *?* in the box.

I like pizza[ ]

7. Circle the word that is the adjective.

The hungry boy munched the sandwich.

boy hungry munched

8. Write *faster* or *fastest*.

A cheetah is one of the [ ] animals.

a b c d e f g h i j k l m
n o p q r s t u v w x y z

MY SCORE

Day 4

1. Add the missing letter.

q  s t u

2. Circle the word that comes first in alphabetical order.

ball fish zoo

3. Add ***ea*** and sound out each word.

bch spk

4. Circle the two rhyming words.

mate meet date

5. Write ***am*** or ***is***.

I  *not feeling well.*

6. Write **.** or ***?*** in the box.

The telephone is ringing ☐

7. Circle the adjective that describes the ***man***.

The angry man screamed.

8. Add ***er*** or ***est*** to the adjective.

This slice is small ☐ *than that one.*

a b c d e f g h i j k l m
n o p q r s t u v w x y z

MY SCORE

Day 5

WEEK 10

1. Add the missing letter.

 w x y z

2. Circle the word that comes first in alphabetical order.

sad happy angry

3. Correct the spelling mistake.

The artist came in first plase.

4. one glass, two ☐

5. Write ***rode*** or ***road***.

They ☐ *their bikes on the path.*

6. Write **.** or ***?*** in the box.

Can you hear that noise ☐

7. Circle the word that is the adjective.

The beautiful butterfly is flying.

flying beautiful butterfly

8. Write ***colder*** or ***coldest***.

Yesterday was the ☐ *day of the year.*

a b c d e f g h i j k l m
n o p q r s t u v w x y z

MY SCORE

Skill focus

Conjunctions

Sentences are made from many different words. Some words join other words and sentences together. These are known as **conjunctions**.

Here are some conjunctions (joining words):

Look at how they join the words in these sentences:

*My cat is black **and** white.*

*We will be having chicken **or** fish for dinner.*

*I like carrots, **but** I hate beans.*

Practice questions

1. Circle the conjunction (joining word).
   (a) *I was tired and hungry after school.*
   (b) *Should I wear my brown shoes or my black shoes?*
   (c) *I want to play with my friend, but she isn't home.*

2. Write ***and*** or ***or***.
   (a) *My scarf is red* ☐ *yellow.*
   (b) *Should I eat an apple* ☐ *a pear?*

Day 1

1. Write ***but*** or ***and***.
   My aunt read a book to my sister ☐ me.

2. Circle the conjunction (joining word).
   Can we play hide and seek?

3. Correct the spelling mistake.
   Do you know wen we can go to the park?
   ☐ n e wh

4. Circle the word that comes first in alphabetical order.
   fish bird insect

5. Circle the opposite of ***after***.
   around begin before

6. Write **.** or **?** in the box.
   What is your favourite animal ☐

7. Circle the adjective.
   The sky had dark clouds.

8. Circle the two nouns.
   The dog is digging a hole.

Day 2

1. Write ***but*** or ***or***.

   I like juice, ______ only when it is fresh.

2. Circle the conjunction (joining word).

   Would you like to watch TV or read a book?

3. Add ***ee*** or ***ea***.

   My ch____ks have turned red.

4. Circle the word that comes first in alphabetical order.

   car boat truck

5. Which word means the same as ***quick***?

   run slow fast

6. Correct the mistake in the sentence.

   Dad said i can go to the swimming pool.

7. Circle the adjective.

   Mum poured hot gravy into a jug.

8. Write the two nouns.

   The goldfish swam around in the tank.

Day 3

1. Write ***or*** or ***but***.

   Dad wanted to make dinner, ______ Mum had already cooked it.

2. Circle the conjunction (joining word).

   I stroked the cat gently, but he scratched me.

3. Correct the spelling mistake.

   Our class goes to the library tooday.

4. Circle the word that comes first in alphabetical order.

   apple orange plum

5. Circle the opposite of ***sink***.

   swim float waves

6. Write **.** or **?** in the box.

   When are we going to the park

7. Circle the adjective.

   The fly got caught in a sticky web.

8. Circle the two nouns.

   The boys are kicking the football.

WEEK 11

WEEK 11

Day 4

1. Write ***but*** or ***and***.

   I want to go to the cinema [ ] *the park.*

2. Circle the conjunction (joining word).

   I like to draw unicorns and dragons.

3. Add ***ee*** or ***ea***.

   I like m[ ]t and vegetables.

4. Circle the word that comes first in alphabetical order.

   potato carrot beans

5. The word ***middle*** means the:

   end centre edge

6. Correct the mistake in the sentence.

   when is it time to go to the party?

7. Circle the adjective.

   The thief had brown hair.

8. Write the two nouns.

   Please put the plate on the table.

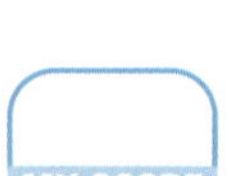

Day 5

1. Write ***but*** or ***or***.

   I will wear my pink dress [ ] *my blue dress.*

2. Circle the conjunction (joining word).

   Is your mum or your dad picking you up from school?

3. Correct the spelling mistake.

   I have the moste toys.

   [ ] s t m o

4. Circle the word that comes first in alphabetical order.

   cloud sky rain

5. Circle the opposite of ***near***.

   far here where

6. Write **.** or **?** in the box.

   The school bus is late [ ]

7. Circle the adjective.

   A giraffe has a long neck.

8. Circle the two nouns.

   I saw crumbs on the carpet.

Skill focus

How is it done?

Sentences are made from many different words. Words that tell us what someone or something is doing are called **verbs**.

Some words tell us how the verb happened. These are known as **adverbs**.

These words often end in ***ly***.

The lady rode her bike safely. *The lady rode her bike dangerously.*

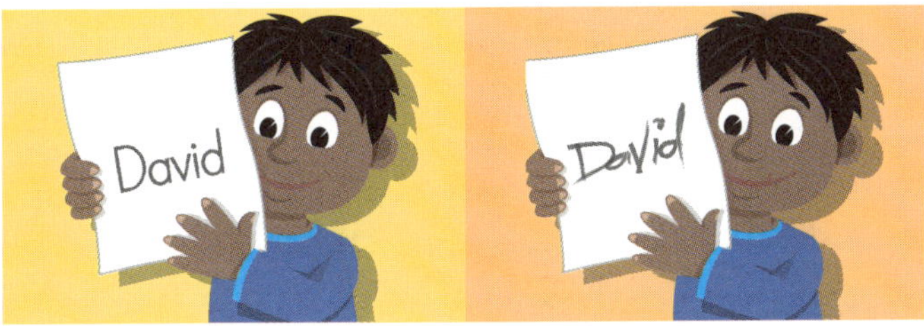

David wrote his name carefully. *David wrote his name carelessly.*

These words help us understand how the action was done.

Practice questions

1. Circle the word that tells how the breeze blew.

   wind blew gently

   The breeze blew gently.

2. Circle the word that tells how the dog panted.

   dog panted noisily

   The dog panted noisily.

Day 1

1. Add ***ly*** to ***strong*** to make a new word.

2. Which word tells how the girl dived?

   girl ☐ safely ☐ pool ☐

   The girl dived safely into the pool.

3. Write the jumbled word correctly.

   I need to ochp the wood for the fire.

4. Circle the word that comes last in alphabetical order.

   river sea lake

5. Circle the word you can add to ***egg***.

   chick shell yellow

6. Add two capital letters.

   is your birthday in october?

7. Write ***or*** or ***and***.

   I can see a cow ____ a sheep.

8. Are the underlined words nouns or adjectives?

   He has shiny, black shoes.

   nouns ☐

   adjectives ☐

Day 2

1. Add *ly* to *safe* to make a new word.

2. Which word tells how the girl looked?

   sadly ☐ out ☐ window ☐

   The girl looked sadly out the window.

3. Add *oo* and sound out each word.

   g☐se sp☐n

4. Add *s* or *es* to change the verb. *Hint: The rules for adding **s** or **es** to verbs are the same as plural nouns.*

   He catch☐ the ball with two hands.

5. Write *was* or *were*.

   They ☐ going for a swim.

6. This sentence is missing something. Correct it.

   I really want to see the film

7. Circle the conjunction (joining word).

   Tom likes apples and so does Taj.

8. Are the underlined words nouns or adjectives?

   The parrot has green and red feathers.

   nouns adjectives

MY SCORE

Day 3

1. Add *ly* to *sad* to make a new word.

2. Which word tells how the girl walked?

   walked ☐ slowly ☐ hill ☐

   She walked slowly up the hill.

3. Write the jumbled word correctly.

   Your nich is under your lip.

4. Circle the word that comes last in alphabetical order.

   desk chair table

5. Which word can you add to *sand*?

   beach white castle

6. Add two capital letters.

   mr johnson is my neighbour.

7. Write *and* or *but*.

   It is sunny now, ☐ it will rain later.

8. Are the underlined words nouns or adjectives?

   I ate a ripe banana and a purple plum.

   nouns adjectives

MY SCORE

Day 4

1. Add ***ly*** to ***slow*** to make a new word.

2. Which word tells how the man laughed?

   loudly ☐ at ☐ joke ☐

   The man laughed loudly at the joke.

3. Add ***oo*** and sound out each word.

   fd tth

4. Add ***s*** or ***es*** to change the verb.

   The baby play ☐ with a rattle.

5. Write ***was*** or ***were***.

   Sam ☐ reading a book.

6. This sentence is missing something. Correct it.

   What is his name

7. Circle the conjunction (joining word).

   We were going to play outside, but it was raining.

8. Are the underlined words nouns or adjectives?

   That little dog has the loudest bark.

   nouns adjectives

Day 5

1. Add ***ly*** to ***loud*** to make a new word.

2. Which word tells how the boy ran?

   boy ☐ quickly ☐ hill ☐

   The boy ran quickly down the hill.

3. Write the jumbled word correctly.

   Don't ptir over the toy on the floor.

4. Circle the word that comes last in alphabetical order.

   brick wood steel

5. Circle the word you can add to ***door***.

   bell window key

6. Add two capital letters.

   the month of november has 30 days.

7. Write ***or*** or ***and***.

   Is the coat Tina's ☐ Jade's?

8. Are the underlined words nouns or adjectives?

   The happy bird flew off into the cloudy sky.

   nouns adjectives

WEEK 12

Skill focus

Making words shorter

Sometimes two words can be put together to make a new, shorter word. These are known as **contractions**.

A letter is taken out and a little mark shows where the letter was. The little mark looks like this:

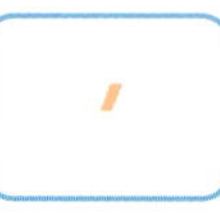

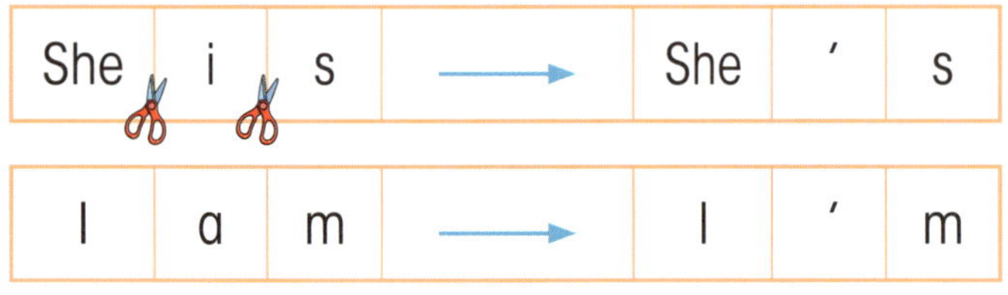

Practice questions

1. Circle the five words that have been made shorter.

2. Write the two words each word is made from.

	+	
	+	
	+	
	+	
	+	

Day 1

1. The word ***don't*** means:

   did not do not

2. Make the contraction (shortened word) ***isn't*** into two words.

3. Write the jumbled word correctly.

   Use uegl to stick it together.

4. Circle the word that comes last in alphabetical order.

   neck finger head

5. The word ***many*** means:

   none not any lots

6. Add two capital letters.

   the largest continent is asia.

7. Which word tells how the boy is writing?

   boy ☐ book ☐ neatly ☐

   The boy is writing neatly in his book.

8. Circle the conjunction (joining word).

   I hate eating cabbage and cucumber.

Day 2

1. The word ***can't*** means:

   cannot   cant   not

2. Make the contraction (shortened word) ***don't*** into two words.

   [ ] [ ]

3. Add ***ew*** and sound out each word.

   n[ ]s   gr[ ]

4. Add ***s*** or ***es*** to change the verb.

   The baby sleep[ ] in her cot.

5. Circle the opposite of ***bottom***.

   over   top   under

6. Write ***.*** or ***?*** in the box.

   What's the time[ ]

7. Circle the better verb.

   The duck walked/ waddled down the path.

8. Which word tells how she goes to school?

   goes ☐   school ☐   happily ☐

   She goes to school happily every day.

Day 3

1. The word ***we're*** means:

   we are   we will

2. Make the contraction (shortened word) ***can't*** into two words.

   [ ] [ ]

3. Write the jumbled word correctly.

   Do you know ywh they are late?

   [ ]

4. Circle the word that comes last in alphabetical order.

   hot   warm   cold

5. Circle the word that means the same as ***cross***.

   loud   happy   angry

6. Add four capital letters.

   new year's day is in january.

7. Which word tells how Harry gets out of the chair?

   gets ☐   chair ☐   slowly ☐

   Harry gets out of the chair slowly.

8. Use the conjunction (joining word) ***or*** or ***and***.

   Choose a plum [ ] a banana, but you can't have both.

WEEK 13

Day 4

1. The word ***hasn't*** means:

   has not   have not

2. Make the contraction (shortened word) ***we're*** into two words.

3. Add ***ew*** and sound out each word.

   thr___   j___els

4. Add ***s*** or ***es*** to change the verb.

   She brush___ her teeth carefully.

5. Circle the opposite of ***pull***.

   move   drag   push

6. Write **.** or **?** in the box.

   How do you know that___

7. Circle the better verb.

   Dad cooked/baked a cake.

8. Which word tells how the children were eating?

   children   eating   greedily

   The children were eating greedily.

Day 5

1. The word ***I'm*** means:

   I am   I will

2. Make the contraction (shortened word) ***hasn't*** into two words.

3. Write the jumbled word correctly.

   The plant will gwro into a small tree.

4. Circle the word that comes last in alphabetical order.

   fish   dolphin   shark

5. Circle the word that means the same as ***cry***.

   sad   laugh   weep

6. Add two capital letters.

   I love christmas day.

7. Which word tells how the baby is crying?

   baby   crying   loudly

   The baby is crying loudly.

8. Circle the conjunction (joining word).

   I climbed the hill but it was hard to do.

Skill focus

Other words for people or things

Some words can be used instead of the names of people and things.

I	me	it	they
them	him	her	

When we use these words, we must make sure they match.

<u>He</u> kicked the ball. The man shouted at <u>him</u>. (<u>He</u> and <u>him</u> match.)

<u>They</u> like to run. It keeps <u>them</u> healthy. (<u>They</u> and <u>them</u> match.)

We can also use words like these to show who something belongs to:

yours	ours	theirs
mine	hers	his

Abby has a new bike. It is <u>hers</u>.

That dog is our dog. It is <u>ours</u>.

Practice questions

1. Is this sentence correct?

   yes ☐ no ☐

   Mum said it was her skirt.

2. Write ***its*** or ***theirs***.

   Tommy and John played with the ball.

   It is ☐.

Day 1

1. Write ***I*** or ***me***.

   Do you think ☐ *can do this?*

2. Write ***his*** or ***hers***.

   It is Jack's birthday cake. The cake is ☐.

3. Correct the spelling mistake.

   Can you <u>sho</u> me your homework?

   ☐ <u>ow</u> <u>sh</u>

4. Circle the word that comes second in alphabetical order.

   bed pillow rug

5. Write ***blue*** or ***blew***.

   My favourite colour is ☐.

6. The contraction (shortened word) ***isn't*** means:

   is not has not

7. Circle the word that tells how Dad pushed the swing.

   Dad pushed the swing gently.

8. Use the (joining word) ***or*** or ***and***.

   He washed the car ☐ *mowed the lawn.*

WEEK 14

Day 2

1. Write ***It*** or ***They***.

   I have a pet. ________ is a cat.

2. Write ***ours*** or ***theirs***.

   The rabbits are in the hutch. It is ________.

3. Add ***oo*** or ***ew***.

   The g____se laid an egg.

4. Add ***s*** or ***es*** to change the verb.

   Dad wash____ the dog on Sundays.

5. Write ***has*** or ***have***.

   Molly ________ a sore thumb.

6. Which word means ***has not***?

   hasn't   *haven't*

7. Pick the better verb: ***laughed*** or ***spoke***.

   The teacher ________ crossly.

8. Circle the conjunction (joining word).

   I like summer, but I don't like winter.

MY SCORE

Day 3

1. Write ***I*** or ***me***.

   My dog loves to play with ________.

2. Write ***his*** or ***hers***.

   That girl has a flower. The flower is ________.

3. Correct the spelling mistake.

   Where duz your aunt live?

   ________ d s oe

4. Circle the word that comes second in alphabetical order.

   finger   *toe*   *leg*

5. Write ***sail*** or ***sale***.

   The wind will blow the ________.

6. The contraction (shortened word) ***I'm*** means:

   I am   *I have*

7. Circle the word that tells how the class is working.

   The class is working quietly.

8. Use the conjunction (joining word) ***or*** or ***but***.

   I don't like spiders ________ snakes.

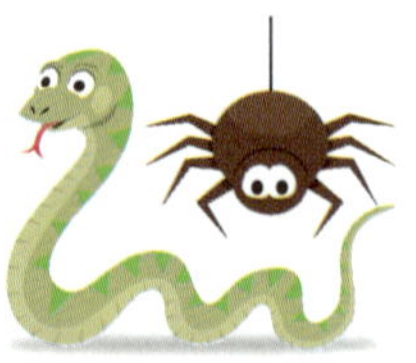

MY SCORE

Day 4

1. Write ***It*** or ***They***.

   The girls are talking. ______ *are noisy.*

2. Write ***mine*** or ***theirs***.

   I have lots of birds. The birds are ______.

3. Add ***oo*** or ***ew***.

   *The pirate and his cr*______ *got lost.*

4. Add ***s*** or ***es*** to change the verb.

   *Mum mow*______ *the lawn on Fridays.*

5. Write ***has*** or ***have***.

   Tom and Tim ______ *bad colds.*

6. Which word means ***I will***?

   I'm I'll

7. Pick the better verb: ***questioned*** or ***answered***.

   Maria ______ *the phone.*

8. Circle the conjunction (joining word).

   He made his bed and he tidied his room.

Day 5

1. Write ***I*** or ***me***.

   Could ______ *have one of those pencils?*

2. Write ***his*** or ***hers***.

   Here are Tim's keys. They are ______.

3. Correct the spelling mistake.

   Four is an eaven number.

   ______

4. Circle the word that comes second in alphabetical order.

   sun moon planet

5. Write ***road*** or ***rode***.

   I live at the end of the ______.

6. The contraction (shortened word) ***don't*** means:

   do not did not

7. Circle the word that tells how the teacher spoke.

   The teacher spoke loudly.

8. Use the conjunction (joining word) ***or*** or ***but***.

   She tried the soup ______ *it was too salty.*

Skill focus

Making opposites

Prefix *un-*

Sometimes, ***un*** can be added to the beginning of words to make a new word.

Adding ***un*** changes the meaning of the word. It makes the word into its opposite!

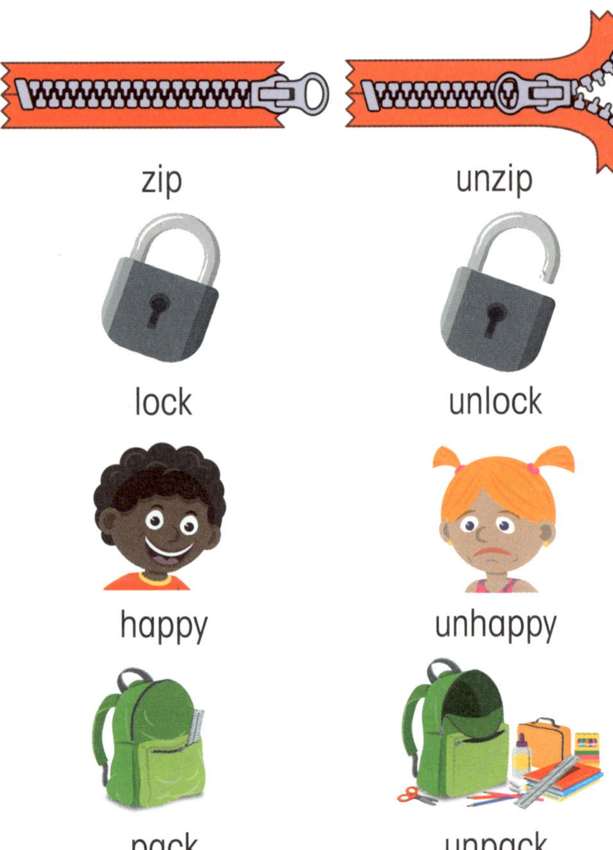

Practice questions

1. Add ***un*** to one word to make the opposite.

   kind bad fun

2. Circle the picture that matches the new word you made.

Day 1

1. Add ***un*** to one word to make the opposite.

   silly happy good

2. Circle the picture that matches the new word you made.

3. Correct the spelling mistake.

   I live in a big howse.

   ou se h

4. Circle the word that comes second in alphabetical order.

   wind cloud rain

5. Which word can you put before ***fall***?

   table water tree

6. Circle the letter left out when we shorten ***does not*** to ***doesn't***.

   a o t

7. Circle the two nouns.

   My cat is licking its paws.

8. Write ***his*** or ***hers***.

   This is Mum's bag. It is ______.

Day 2

1. Add ***un*** to one word to make the opposite.

   well sit eat

2. Circle the picture that matches the new word you made.

3. Add ***ea*** or ***ee*** and ***oo*** or ***ew***.

   The water will fr☐ze in that cold r☐m.

4. Add ***s*** or ***es*** to change the verb.

   Mum water☐ the plants every day.

5. Write ***seen*** or ***saw***.

   We have ☐ that film.

6. The contraction (shortened word) ***I've*** means:

   I have I am

7. Are the underlined words nouns or verbs?

   Some <u>muffins</u> are in the <u>oven</u>.

   nouns verbs

8. Write ***She*** or ***Her***.

   ☐ dropped the pencil on the floor.

MY SCORE

Day 3

1. Add ***un*** to one word to make the opposite.

   skip lock talk

2. Circle the picture that matches the new word you made.

3. Correct the spelling mistake.

   What do you <u>nead</u> to pack for your holiday?

   d ee n

4. Circle the word that comes second in alphabetical order.

   kettle pot toaster

5. Which word can you put before ***stick***?

   mat stone broom

6. Circle the letter left out to make the contraction (shortened word) ***haven't***.

   a i o

7. Circle the two nouns.

   Pass me the salt and pepper.

8. Write ***He*** or ***She***.

   Ken is my brother.

   ☐ is a boy.

MY SCORE

Day 4

1. Add ***un*** to one word to make the opposite.

   brush load swim

2. Circle the picture that matches the new word you made.

3. Add ***oo*** or ***ew*** and ***ea*** or ***ee***.

   The wind bl [ ] the l[ ]ves off the tree.

4. Add ***s*** or ***es*** to change the verb.

   The bee buzz[ ] around the flower.

5. Write ***seen*** or ***saw***.

   We [ ] a spider on its web.

6. The contraction (shortened word) ***won't*** means:

   would not will not

7. Is the underlined word a noun or adjective?

   The frightened puppy ran away.

   noun adjective

8. Write ***Him*** or ***He***.

   [ ] picked up the apple core.

MY SCORE

Day 5

1. Add ***un*** to one word to make the opposite.

   shoe kick tie

2. Circle the picture that matches the new word you made.

3. Correct the spelling mistake.

   Do you know the ansa to this problem?

   [ ] a s wer n

4. Circle the word that comes second in alphabetical order.

   small little tiny

5. Circle the word you can add to ***every***.

   some never thing

6. Circle the letters left out to make the contraction (shortened word) ***we've***.

   he ha we

7. Circle the two nouns.

   The butterfly is on the leaf.

8. Write ***He*** or ***She***.

   Daniel is my brother.

   [ ] is six.

MY SCORE

Day 1

1. Correct the spelling mistake.

The snow is wite.

i e wh t

2. Add ***oo*** or ***ew*** and ***ea*** or ***ee***.

The rare j____els were the prettiest I had s____n.

3. Number the words in alphabetical order.

pink ☐ green ☐ black ☐

4. Add ***un*** to one word to make the opposite.

fair bad little

5. Write ***sun*** or ***son***.

His ____ is called Dylan.

6. Circle the word that means the same as ***chop***.

cut roll chew

7. Write **.**, **!** or **?** in the box.

How are you feeling ☐

8. Circle the word that tells how the cat ate.

My cat ate greedily.

MY SCORE

Day 2

1. Write the jumbled word correctly.

There is a dirty otps on your shirt.

2. Add ***ea*** or ***ee*** and ***oo*** or ***ew***.

We are going to s____ a film s____n.

3. Number the words in alphabetical order.

ant ☐ spider ☐ beetle ☐

4. Add ***ed*** or ***ing***.

Connor pick____ a pretty flower for his mum.

5. Shorten ***I am*** into one word.

6. Write ***sun*** or ***son***.

The ____ is behind a cloud.

7. Circle the conjunction (joining word).

Mum likes chocolate and Dad likes it too.

8. Write the correct word.

I Me

My name is Oscar.

____ am a boy.

MY SCORE

WEEK 16

Day 3

1. Correct the spelling mistake.

   Can you tel the time?

ll t e

2. Add ***ea*** or ***ee*** and ***oo*** or ***ew***.

   I went to sl*p in my n bed.*

3. Number in alphabetical order.

   sand

   beach

   waves

4. Add ***un*** to one word to make the ***opposite***.

   buy do it

5. Write ***one*** or ***won***.

   I have  *turn left.*

6. Circle the opposite of ***here***.

   where there come

7. Write **.**, ***!*** or ***?*** in the box.

   Wow

8. Circle the word that tells how the sun was shining.

   The sun was shining brightly.

Day 4

1. Write the jumbled word correctly.

   I can't wait until your birthday prtya.

2. Add ***ea*** or ***ee*** and ***oo*** or ***ew***.

   The sh p were eating their f d.

3. Number in alphabetical order.

   foot toe hand

4. Add ***ed*** or ***ing***.

   We are walk home from school today.

5. Shorten ***did not*** into one word.

6. Write ***one*** or ***won***.

   My sister the race.

7. Circle the conjunction (joining word).

   I can't find my book, but I found my pencil.

8. Circle the correct word.

   I me

   The teacher smiled at .

Day 5

1. Correct the spelling mistake.

   I am not shure where I left my shoes.

   ure s

2. Add ***ea*** or ***ee*** and ***oo*** or ***ew***.

   Dad added some m___t to the st___.

3. Number in alphabetical order.

   long ☐ short ☐ thin ☐

4. Add ***un*** to one word to make the opposite.

   even walk bump

5. Circle the word that means the same as ***fix***.

   mend rip drop

6. Circle the opposite of ***black***.

   brown white gold

7. Write **.** or **?** in the box.

   Could I use your ball ☐

8. Circle the word that tells how he won the race.

   He won the race easily.

Skill focus review

1. Correct the spelling mistake.

   What is your favourite TV sho?

   ow sh

2. Number in alphabetical order.

   tree ☐ leaf ☐ flower ☐

3. Add ***un*** to one word to make the opposite.

   friendly sleep run

4. The contraction (shortened word) ***you're*** means:

   you are *you will*

5. Circle the conjunction (joining word).

   I like my friend but he can be rude to me.

6. Circle the correct word.

   I me

   Do you want to go to the pool with ______?

7. Write the correct word.

   she he

   Dad said ______ would pick me up from school.

8. Circle the word that tells how she is singing.

   She is singing beautifully.

Skill focus

Verbs with two parts

Some verbs (doing words) can be in a group of two. These are called verb groups.

*The girl **had played** all day.*

*The boy **is counting**.*

Verb groups and the endings of verbs tell us when something happens.

This is called **tense**.

Past tense

Actions that have already happened often end with ***ed***.

The verb group usually has the word ***was*** or ***were*** and a verb that ends with ***ing***:

*My mum **was reading** her book late last night.*

Present tense

Actions that are happening now usually end with ***s*** or ***ing***.

The verb group usually has the word ***am***, ***is*** or ***are*** and a verb that ends with ***ing***:

*My dad **is cooking** dinner for us.*

Practice questions

1. Circle the two words that make the verb group.
   (a) The sun is shining today.
   (b) We are staying with Dad.
2. Is the sentence in the past or present tense?
   (a) My aunt stayed with us at the weekend.
   past present
   (b) The children are playing with the dog.
   past present

Day 1

1. Circle the two words that make the verb group.
   The girl is swimming all the way.
2. Is the sentence in the past tense or present tense?
   I was washing my hair.
   past present
3. Correct the spelling mistake.
   Would you like anuther bowl of soup?
   [ ] er th a n o
4. Number in alphabetical order.
   Liam [ ] Grace [ ] Tanya [ ]
5. Circle the word that means the same as ***stop***.
   go finish move
6. Add ***un*** to one word to make the opposite.
   have likely ride
   [ ]
7. Write **.**, **!** or **?** in the box.
   The clown made us laugh [ ]
8. Write the correct word: ***it*** or ***them***.

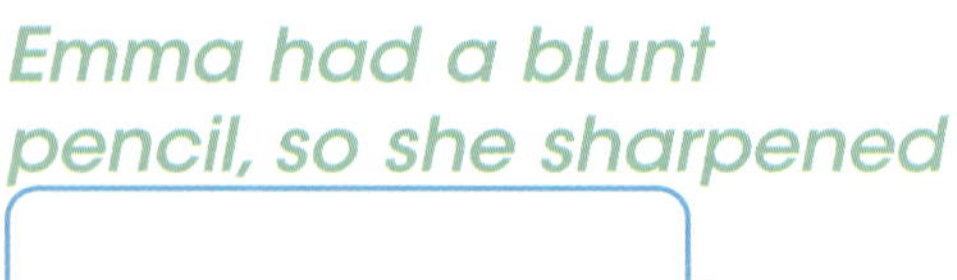

Emma had a blunt pencil, so she sharpened [ ].

Day 2

1. Circle the two words that make the verb group.

   The dog was digging a big hole.

2. Is the sentence in the past tense or present tense?

   A man is fishing at the lake.

   past present

3. Add ***oi*** and sound out each word.

   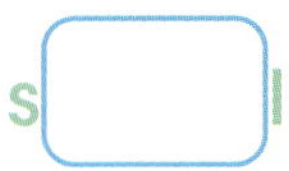 s[ ]l 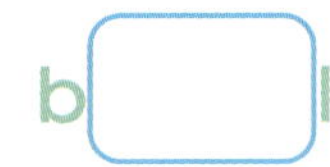 b[ ]l

4. Number in alphabetical order.

   lamb  foal  cub 

5. Circle the opposite of ***under***.

   inside over behind

6. Add ***ed*** or ***ing***.

   The boy look[ ] for his ball over the fence.

7. Add two capital letters and a full stop.

   mr bishop has his car in the garage

8. Circle the word that tells how the moon shone.

   The moon shone brightly in the sky.

MY SCORE

Day 3

1. Circle the two words that make the verb group.

   Dad is fixing the gate.

2. Is the sentence in the past tense or present tense?

   Last night, the dog chased the cat.

   past present

3. Correct the spelling mistake.

   Do you know wherre he lives?

   [ ] ere wh

4. Number in alphabetical order.

   sand [ ] dirt [ ] rocks [ ]

5. Circle the word which means the same as ***enormous***.

   tiny strong huge

6. Add ***un*** to one word to make the opposite.

   skip lock talk

   [ ]

7. Write **.**, **!** or **?** in the box.

   Are you scared of spiders[ ]

8. Choose the correct word.

   He She

   Anna is my best friend.

   [ ] *sits next to me.*

MY SCORE

WEEK 17

Day 4

1. Circle the two words that make the verb group.

   The sun is shining today.

2. Is the sentence in the past tense or present tense?

   They are drawing pictures.

   past present

3. Add ***oy*** and sound out each word.

   enj☐ ☐ster

4. Number in alphabetical order.

   bed ☐ pillow ☐ rug ☐

5. Circle the opposite of ***messy***.

   tidy untidy smelly

6. Add ***ed*** or ***ing***.

   The children were talk☐ loudly about their holidays.

7. Add two capital letters and a question mark.

   where did you hide the christmas present

8. Write the word that describes how the robber moved.

   The robber moved silently in the house.

MY SCORE

Day 5

1. Circle the two words that make the verb group.

   We are staying with our cousins.

2. Is the sentence in the past tense or present tense?

   All the children passed their test.

   past present

3. Correct the spelling mistake.

   I learnt to swim wen I was four.

   ☐ n wh e

4. Number in alphabetical order.

   cry ☐ laugh ☐ sneeze ☐

5. Circle the word that means the same as ***wealthy***.

   old rich poor

6. Add ***un*** to one word to make the opposite.

   pack walk cry

7. Write **.**, **!** or **?** in the box.

   My baby sister has learnt to crawl☐

8. Write the correct word: ***it*** or ***him***.

   When James fell off his bike, Dad helped ☐ *get up again.*

MY SCORE

Teeth not tooths

The word we use for *more than one* person or thing is called a **plural**.

When we have *only one* of something, it is called a **singular**.

To make a plural, we usually add ***s*** or ***es***.

Sometimes, when there is more than one person or thing, the whole word changes.

We do not add ***s*** or ***es*** to the end of the word.

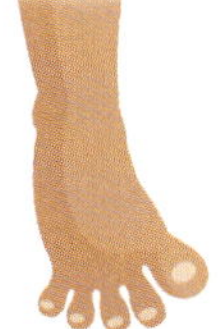
One foot

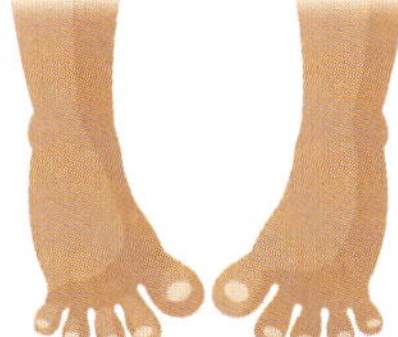
Two feet

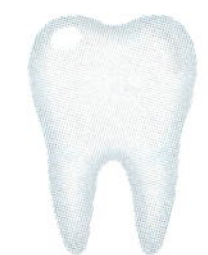
One tooth

Lots of teeth

One child

A class of children

Some words, like sheep, always stay the same even when there is more than one.

Look at the lonely sheep. He isn't standing with the other sheep.

Practice questions

1. Circle the plural of ***child***.

   childs   childes   children

2. Write the singular of ***teeth***.

   [ ]

---

1. Circle the plural of ***man***.

   mans   mens   men

2. Write the singular of ***children***.

   two children

   one [ ]

3. Correct the spelling mistake.

   I live neer the bus stop.

   [ ] ea r n

4. Write the plural of ***church***.

   [ ]

5. Circle the word you can add to ***after***.

   before   noon   now

6. What does the contraction (shortened word) ***I've*** mean?

   I've got to go home at six.

   [ ]

7. Write ***is*** or ***are***.

   Peter [ ] *sure he got the answer right.*

8. Is the sentence in the past tense or present tense?

   The girls are playing a game.

   past   present

Day 2

1. Circle the plural of ***person***.

   people   persones   peoples

2. Write the singular of ***men***.

   two men

   one

3. Add ***oi*** or ***oy***.

   The t____s were all over the floor.

4. Add ***s*** or ***es*** to change the verb.

   At school, the boy miss____ his mum very much.

5. Add ***right*** or ***write***.

   Look to the left and ____.

6. Add two capital letters.

   my favourite month is december.

7. Circle the two words that make the verb group.

   I am eating my lunch.

8. Is the sentence in the past tense or present tense?

   I watched television last night.

   past   present

MY SCORE

Day 3

1. Circle the plural of ***woman***.

   womans   womenes   women

2. Write the singular of ***people***.

   two people

   one

3. Correct the spelling mistake.

   What is your house numba?

   er n u b m

4. Write the plural of ***kiss***.

5. Circle the word you can add to ***in***.

   table   go   side

6. What does the contraction (shortened word) ***it's*** mean?

   I think it's going to rain tomorrow.

7. Write ***is*** or ***are***.

   Mum and Dad ____ going to a hotel.

8. Is the sentence in the past tense or present tense?

   A butterfly is fluttering above us.

   past   present

Day 4

1. Circle the plural of ***foot***.

foots feets feet

2. Write the singular of ***women***.

two women

one [ ]

3. Add ***oi*** or ***oy***.

I found a gold c[ ]n at the beach.

4. Add ***s*** or ***es*** to change the verb.

My dad teach[ ] me how to fix cars.

5. Add ***write*** or ***right***.

I [ ] with my left hand.

6. Add two capital letters.

My friend asked if i could go to her party on saturday.

7. Circle the two words that make the verb group.

The bird has made a small nest.

8. Is the sentence in the past tense or present tense?

Jack jumped on the trampoline after school.

past present

Day 5

WEEK 18

1. Circle the plural of ***mouse***.

mouses mice mices

2. Write the singular of ***feet***.

two feet

one [ ]

3. Correct the spelling mistake.

The rude bus driver was very meen.

[ ] ea m n

4. Write the plural of ***fox***.

[ ]

5. Circle the word you can add to ***some***.

come thing when

6. What does the contraction (shortened word) ***that's*** mean?

We know that's the right answer.

[ ]

7. Write ***is*** or ***are***.

If we [ ] quiet, we can go outside.

8. Is the sentence in the past tense or present tense?

Dad is watching the TV.

past present

WEEK 19

Skill focus

There or their?

There and ***their*** are two words that are often mixed up.

Even though they sound the same, these words have different meanings.

There

We use there when we are talking about a place.

Look at the dog over there.

There are lots of children at the park.

Their

We use their when something belongs to a group of people or animals.

Their names are Emma and Andy.

They love their new school.

That dog is theirs.

Choosing the right word is important. It helps our sentence make sense.

Practice questions

1. Write ***there*** or ***their***.

   I can't wait to go ______ *on my holiday.*

   I am going to ______ *house after school.*

2. Is the underlined word correct?

   yes ☐ no ☐

   There are four ducks on the pond.

Day 1

1. Write ***there*** or ***their***.

   I would love to go ______.

2. Is the underlined word correct?

   yes ☐ no ☐

   I like playing at their house.

3. Write the jumbled word correctly.

   Your seat is over ehre.

   ______

4. Write the plural of ***man***.

   one man

   two ______

5. Circle the word that rhymes with ***lady***.

   baby shady party

6. Write **.**, **!** or **?** in the box.

   Do you have a pet rabbit ☐

7. Circle the nouns.

   The ladder is in the shed.

8. Circle and write the verb group.

   We are going to the park now.

   ______

Day 2

1. Write ***there*** or ***their***.

   Is that ________ dog?

2. Is the underlined word correct?

   yes ☐ no ☐

   Do you want to go <u>their</u>?

3. Add ***ur*** and sound out each word.

   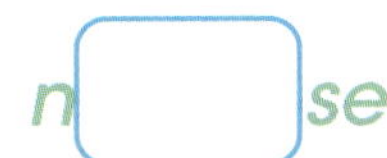

   p____se n____se

4. Add two letters to make the word say the opposite: ***well***.

5. Which word is not a real word?

   bring brang brought

6. Circle the letters left out to make the contraction (shortened word) ***they've***.

   ha hi wi

7. Circle the noun.

   The children are playing nicely.

8. Circle present tense or past tense.

   We were worried because he was late.

   present past

Day 3

1. Write ***there*** or ***their***.

   I saw ________ car in town.

2. Is the underlined word correct?

   yes ☐ no ☐

   Is that your mum over <u>there</u>?

3. Write the jumbled word correctly.

   I wish I <u>cldou</u> fly to the moon.

4. Write the singular of ***mice***.

   two mice

   one

5. Circle the word that does not rhyme with ***high***.

   any reply fly

6. Write **.**, **!** or **?** in the box.

   Ouch ☐ That really hurt.

7. Circle the adjectives.

   Pour the hot gravy on the roast beef.

8. Circle and write the verb group.

   I have finished my homework.

WEEK 19

Day 4

1. Write ***there*** or ***their***.

   The children have cheese in ☐ *sandwiches.*

2. Is the underlined word correct?

   yes ☐ no ☐

   The dogs are wagging there tails.

3. Add ***er*** and sound out each word.

   wint ☐ *fing* ☐

4. Add two letters to make the word say the opposite: ***kind***.

   ☐

5. Write ***bring*** or ***brought***.

   Did you ☐ *your comics to school?*

6. Circle the letters left out to make the contraction (shortened word) ***he'll***.

   wi wa he

7. Circle the noun.

   I won the huge trophy.

8. Circle present tense or past tense.

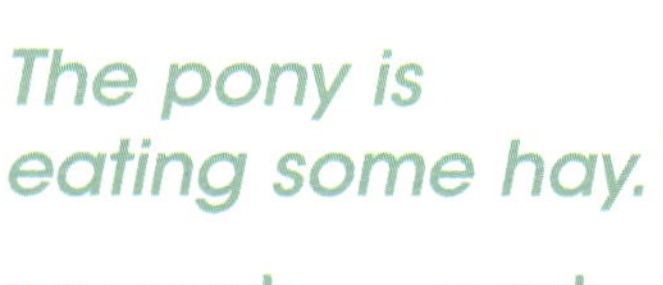

   The pony is eating some hay.

   present past

Day 5

1. Write ***there*** or ***their***.

   The children are in ☐ *classroom.*

2. Is the underlined word correct?

   yes ☐ no ☐

   I like their new car.

3. Write the jumbled word correctly.

   I saw a butterfly in the nrgead.

   ☐

4. Write the plural of ***person***.

   one person

   two ☐

5. Circle the word that rhymes with ***hedge***.

   ridge edge bridge

6. Write **.**, **!** or **?** in the box.

   'How old are you ☐ *' she asked.*

7. Circle the nouns.

   Our house is on a busy street.

8. Circle and write the verb group.

   Our hen has laid an egg.

   ☐

Skill focus

Rules for adding endings (change *y* to *i*)

We can add ***s*** to the end of nouns (naming words) to show that we have more than one.

The dogs are running around the park.

We can add ***s*** to the end of verbs to show that they are happening now.

She plays a game with her friend.

But when words end in ***y***, there are special rules for adding an ***s*** to the end.

If there is a vowel (***a e i o u***) before the ***y***, we just add ***s***.

key *keys*

pay *pays*

When a word ends with a consonant then ***y***, we change the ***y*** to ***i*** and add ***es***.

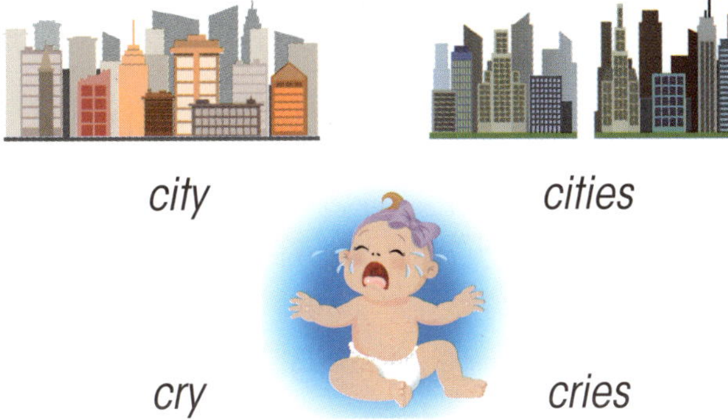

city *cities*

cry *cries*

Practice questions

1. Change the ***y*** to ***i*** and add ***es*** to make this word say more than one.

   one fly, two ______

2. dry + es = ______

Day 1

1. Write the plural of ***baby***.

   ______

2. reply + es = ______

3. Write the jumbled word correctly.

   The opposite of low is ghih.

   ______

4. Write the words in alphabetical order.

   ear nose lip

   ______ ______ ______

5. Write ***there*** or ***their***.

   I'm glad ______ *is more cake!*

6. Circle the mistake.

   I wanted to go for a run, but i hurt my leg.

7. Circle the conjunction (joining word).

   She tried it on, but it was too small.

8. Finish the sentence with ***going*** or ***are going***.

   We ______ *to the zoo on Sunday.*

WEEK 20

Day 2

1. Write the plural of ***lady***.

2. dry + es =

3. Add ***er*** and sound out each word.

numb teach

4. Circle the word that stays the same when singular or plural.

sheep horse fox

5. Write ***meet*** or ***meat***.

We will at the bus stop.

6. Add two capital letters.

my uncle lives in france.

7. Write ***older*** or ***oldest***.

Andrew is the boy in the class.

8. Circle the adjective.

Tim's sister has a tiny room.

Day 3

1. Write the plural of ***cherry***.

2. try + es =

3. Write the jumbled word correctly.

We ouhsld go to bed soon.

4. Write the words in alphabetical order.

zebra deer tiger

5. Write ***their*** or ***there***.

They left lights on.

6. Circle the mistake.

Our family is going on holiday in march.

7. Circle the conjunction (joining word).

I sit next to Meg and Shannon.

8. Finish the sentence with ***playing*** or ***were playing***.

They games at lunchtime.

WEEK 20

Day 4

1. Write the plural of ***berry***.

2. marry + es =

3. Add ***ur*** and sound out each word.

t___key

ch___ch

4. Circle the word that stays the same when singular or plural.

fish whale shark

5. Write ***meet*** or ***meat***.

You buy ___ from a butcher.

6. Add two capital letters.

liam's baby brother is called ethan.

7. Write ***lighter*** or ***lightest***.

A butterfly is

than a snail.

8. Circle the adjective.

Adam loves to eat spicy chicken.

Day 5

1. Write the plural of ***copy***.

2. bunny + es =

3. Write the jumbled word correctly.

Kelly sits in ontfr of me.

4. Write the words in alphabetical order.

long wide thin

5. Write ***their*** or ***there***.

I have not been ___ before.

6. Circle the mistake.

My friend marcus is good at tennis.

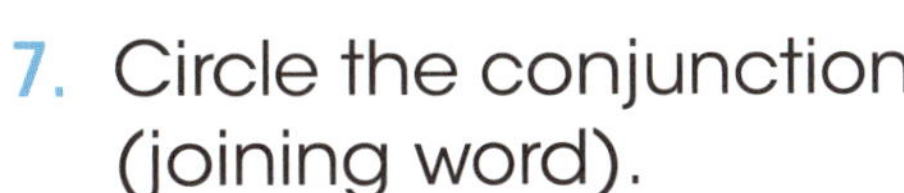
7. Circle the conjunction (joining word).

He looked, but he couldn't find it.

8. Finish the sentence with ***walking*** or ***is walking***.

Maria ___ to school with her friend Leah.

Skill focus

What is a comma?

When we have a list of words, we use commas between each word. A comma looks like this:

,

Look at Gran's shopping list.

We can write this list as a sentence too:

commas

Gran wants milk, soup, fruit cake and soap from the shop.

and between last two words

Every word in the list has a comma between it except the last two.

The word ***and*** goes between the last two words.

Practice questions

1. Circle the comma in each sentence.

   Mia had a doll, football and teddy bear for her birthday.

   Dad cooked sausages, potatoes and peas for dinner.

2. Put a comma (,) in the correct place in each sentence.

   Put on your hat coat and scarf.

   My shirt is red blue and white.

Day 1

1. Circle the comma.

   I like playing football, tennis and basketball.

2. Add one comma (,).

   I hate mice ants and spiders.

3. Correct the spelling mistake.

   I am going on holiday next yeer.

   ea r y

4. Write the words in alphabetical order.

   pencil chalk marker

5. Write the plural of ***party***.

6. Circle the word you can put before ***self***.

   some who your

7. Circle the correct contraction (shortened word).

   don't do'nt

8. Write the better word: ***politely*** or ***rudely***.

   We thanked him ______ *for helping.*

Day 2

1. Circle the comma.

   I will have roast beef, potatoes and peas for dinner.

2. Add one comma (,).

   Pick up your books toys and clothes.

3. Add ***er*** or ***ur***.

   The winn[ ] of the race got a prize.

4. Write the plural of ***family***.

5. Add two letters to make the word say the opposite: ***lock***.

6. Which word can you add to ***some***?

   there   come   times

7. Circle the correct contraction (shortened word).

   we're   wer'e

8. Write ***bought*** or ***brought***.

   We 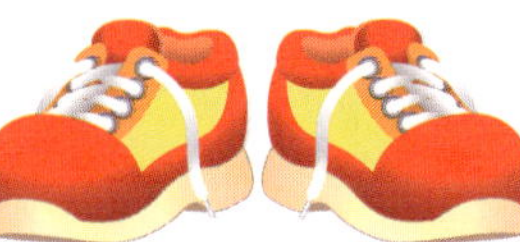 *brand new shoes for the party.*

Day 3

1. Circle the comma.

   My ice cream is strawberry, chocolate and vanilla.

2. Add one comma (,).

   Mum hung out socks shirts and jeans.

3. Correct the spelling mistake.

   I will cawl my aunt on the phone.

ll a c

4. Write the words in alphabetical order.

   hen   rooster   chick

5. fry + es =

6. Circle the word you can put before ***ever***.

   never   how   always

7. Circle the correct contraction (shortened word).

   has'nt   hasn't

8. Write the better word: ***carefully*** or ***carelessly***.

   We crossed the busy road [ ].

WEEK 21

Day 4

1. Circle the comma.

   The Christmas lights are red, green and white.

2. Add one comma (,).

   She drinks milk water and juice.

3. Add ***er*** or ***ur***.

   Sometimes my hair turns c[ ]ly.

4. Write the plural of ***spy***.

5. Add two letters to make the word say the opposite: ***fair***.

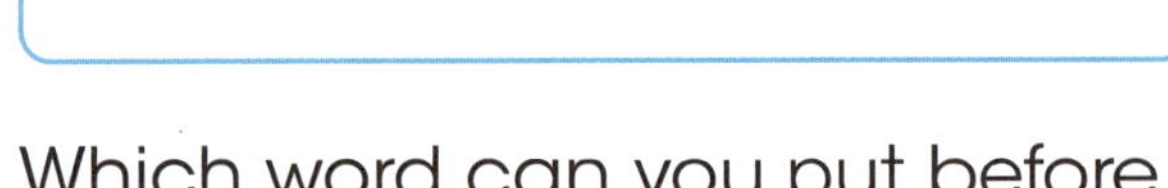

6. Which word can you put before ***one***?

   every boy six

7. Circle the correct contraction (shortened word).

   don't do'nt

8. Write ***bought*** or ***brought***.

   Have you [ ] a warm jacket with you?

Day 5

1. Circle the comma.

   The children travel by car, bus and train.

2. Add one comma (,).

   Sam Tim and Ben are brothers.

3. Correct the spelling mistake.

   Can you help me spell this wurd?

   [ ] or w d

4. Write the words in alphabetical order.

   water soap towel

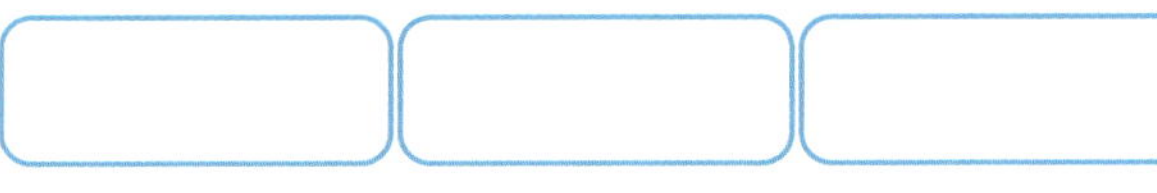

5. Write the plural of ***hobby***.

6. Circle the word you can add to ***out***.

   in side around

7. Circle the correct contraction (shortened word).

   ca'nt can't

8. Write the better word: ***quickly*** or ***slowly***.

   The rabbit ran away [ ] from the fox.

MY SCORE

MY SCORE

Skill focus

Word families

Look at these groups of words:

<u>wash</u>: washes, washed, washing, unwashed

<u>start</u>: starts, started, starting

<u>play</u>: plays, played, playing

These are **word families**.

They are groups of words that can be built from the same word.

Word families help make spelling easier because they help you spell other words in the same family.

Practice questions

1. Add ***ed*** and ***ing*** to make a word family. ***talk***

   ______ ______

2. ***Cooks***, ***cooked*** and ***cooking*** are made from the word ______.

Day 1

1. Add ***ed*** and ***ing*** to make a word family.

   start______ start______

2. ***Smells***, ***smelled*** and ***smelling*** are made from the word ______.

3. Correct the spelling mistake.

   Can I have a <u>tern</u> on the swing?

4. Circle the word that does not rhyme.

   turn burn hurt

5. Write ***their*** or ***there***.

   Your shoe is over ______.

6. Put a comma in the correct place.

   Bread rice and meat are foods.

7. Circle the better verb.

   The phone called/ rang loudly.

8. Write ***looked*** or ***is looking***.

   Dad ______ *really smart in his new shirt yesterday.*

Day 2

1. Add ***ed*** and ***ing*** to make a word family.

   smell____ smell____

2. ***Helps***, ***helped*** and ***helping*** are made from the word ____.

3. Add ***oi*** or ***oy*** and ***ur*** or ***er***.

   The f____l was b____nt in the oven.

4. Circle the word that means ***afraid***.

   scared happy sad

5. Write ***pear*** or ***pair***.

   I need a new ____ of socks.

6. Put a comma in the correct place.

   Mary Jane and Lisa are friends.

7. Circle present tense or past tense.

   I am watching television.

   present past

8. Write ***am doing*** or ***done***.

   I can't come now as I ____ the dishes.

MY SCORE

Day 3

1. Add ***ed*** and ***ing*** to make a word family.

   help____ help____

2. ***Camps***, ***camped*** and ***camping*** are made from the word ____.

3. Correct the spelling mistake.

   My friend was awaye from school today.

   ____ ay w a

4. Circle the two words that rhyme.

   street stream beat

5. Write ***their*** or ***there***.

   Do you know where they left ____ hat?

6. Put a comma in the correct place.

   I like ducks geese and swans.

7. Circle the better verb.

   The horse jumped/bounced over the wall.

8. Write ***are going*** or ***gone***.

   We ____ to the library today.

Day 4

1. Add ***ed*** and ***ing*** to make a word family.

   camp______ camp______

2. ***Covers***, ***covered*** and ***coverings*** are made from the word ______.

3. Add ***oi*** or ***oy*** and ***ur*** or ***er***.

   The b______ has a little sist______.

4. Circle the opposite of ***buy***.

   sell cost money

5. Write ***pair*** or ***pear***.

   A ______ is a type of fruit.

6. Add two commas.

   The four seasons are spring summer autumn and winter.

7. Circle present tense or past tense.

   Our cat is licking her paws.

   present past

8. Write ***are keeping*** or ***kept***.

   Mum ______ the tools in the shed.

Day 5

1. Add ***ed*** and ***ing*** to make a word family.

   cover______ cover______

2. ***Branches*** and ***branched*** are made from the word ______.

3. Correct the spelling mistake.

   I will tri to get ready on time.

4. Circle the word that does not rhyme.

   little middle riddle

5. Write ***their*** or ***there***.

   The ball rolled over ______.

6. Add two commas.

   My shirt is green red black and blue.

7. Circle the better verb.

   Dad gently pushed/shook the swing.

8. Write ***is growing*** or ***grew***.

   We ______ tomatoes in our garden.

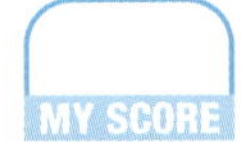

Skill focus

Tricky verbs

Verbs are words that tell us what someone or something is doing.

We usually add ***ed*** to the end of a verb when we want to show that it happened in the past.

Some verbs do not follow this rule.

Instead, we change the whole word when we want to show that it has already happened.

Present	Past	
Please do not break your pencil.	*I broke my pencil.*	
I am watching the flowers grow.	*The flowers grew.*	
Can we eat now?	*We already ate.*	

Practice questions

1. Circle the verb.

   The bird flew onto the branch.

2. Is the sentence in the present tense or past tense?

   The bird flew onto the branch.

   past   present

Day 1

1. Circle the verb.

   My brother broke his arm last week.

2. Is the sentence in the past tense or present tense?

   My brother broke his arm last week.

   past   present

3. Correct the spelling mistake.

   Mum said I can choose one thingk from the dessert list.

   [ ] n g th i

4. Write the words in alphabetical order.

   tea   juice   milk

   [ ] [ ] [ ]

5. ***Spelled*** and ***spelling*** are made from the word [ ].

6. Add a capital letter and a comma.

   today is cold windy and cloudy.

7. Write ***or*** or ***but***.

   Would you like to go to the park [ ] *the pool?*

8. Circle the best noun.

   A rabbit lives in a hedge/burrow/tent.

Day 2

1. Circle the verb.

   The back fence blew down during the storm.

2. Is the sentence in the past tense or present tense?

   The strong wind blew our fence over last night.

   past present

3. Write the missing letter(s). ***wr*** or ***r***

   A circle is a ☐ound shape.

4. Write the plural of ***bully***.

   ☐

5. ***Working*** and ***worked*** are made from the word ☐.

6. Write the correct contraction (shortened word).

   he is = ☐

   he's h'es

7. Circle the correct word.

   That brown shoe is his/him.

8. Write one noun after the clue.

   An insect that spins a web.

   ☐

Day 3

1. Circle the verb.

   The baby slept in the cot.

2. Is the sentence in the past tense or present tense?

   The baby slept in the cot.

   past present

3. Correct the spelling mistake.

   I like bothe of my dogs very much.

   ☐ th b o

4. Write the words in alphabetical order.

   white green orange

   ☐ ☐ ☐

5. ***Brushes*** and ***brushing*** are made from the word ☐.

6. Add a capital letter and a comma.

   Taj Alex and i live on the same street.

7. Write ***but*** or ***and***.

   Please brush your teeth ☐ get dressed.

8. Circle the best noun.

   A king lives in a hut/castle/cabin.

Day 4

1. Circle the verb.

   Mum rang the doctor.

2. Is the sentence in the past tense or present tense?

   Mum rang the doctor.

   past   present

3. Write the missing letter(s). ***wr*** or ***r***

   I can ☐ ite neatly with a sharp pencil.

4. Write the plural of ***pony***.

5. ***Cries*** and ***cried*** are made from the word ☐.

6. Write the correct contraction (shortened word).

   will not = ☐

   wo'nt   won't

7. Circle the correct word.

   Petra said her/she would be late.

8. Write one noun after the clue.

   A yellow fruit that monkeys love.

Day 5

1. Circle the verb.

   We hid under the bed.

2. Is the sentence in the past tense or present tense?

   We hid under the bed so Mum couldn't find us.

   past   present

3. Correct the spelling mistake.

   It will be Christmas soone.

   n oo s

4. Write the words in alphabetical order.

   car   lorry   bus

   ☐ ☐ ☐

5. ***Dries*** and ***dried*** are made from the word ☐.

6. Add one capital letter and a comma.

   did you see the red white and blue shirt?

7. Write ***or*** or ***but***.

   I want to buy a toy, ☐ *I don't have any money.*

8. Circle the best noun.

   The gardener uses a mixer/rake/hairdryer.

WEEK 24

Day 1

1. Correct the spelling mistake.

   Summur is my favourite season.

2. Write the missing letters. ***ork*** or ***alk***

   We had to give a t___ in class.

3. Circle the correct contraction (shortened word).

   we've   wev'e

4. Write ***been*** or ***bean***.

   Have you ___ to the moon?

5. Write the singular of ***berries***.

6. Add two capital letters and a comma.

   i flew to London rome and Sydney last week.

7. Choose the correct word.

   us   them

   We like to jog around the park. Jogging is good for ___.

8. Write the adjective.

   Mum bought lovely flowers.

Day 2

1. Write the jumbled word correctly.

   I write with my htirg hand.

2. Write the missing letter(s). ***w*** or ***wh***

   I waited ___ile Dad went to the office.

3. Write the words in alphabetical order.

   pea   bean   corn

4. Write ***ate*** or ***eight***.

   This flower has ___ petals.

5. ***Tried*** and ***trying*** are made from the word ___.

6. Write **.**, **!** or **?** in the box.

   Do you know how much longer we have to wait___

7. Add one word: ***she*** or ***her***.

   Alice dropped a book so I picked it up for ___.

8. Write ***and*** or ***but***.

   On our holiday we went fishing ___ hiking.

Day 3

1. Correct the spelling mistake.

   We had to giv our dirty dog a bath.

   ve i g

2. Write the missing letters. ***oar*** or ***ore***

   Mr Smith wrote a list on the b[ ]d.

3. Circle the correct contraction (shortened word).

   theyv'e   they've

4. Write ***been*** or ***bean***.

   A [ ] is long and green.

5. Write the plural of ***paintbrush***.

6. Add two capital letters and a comma.

   mrs turner gave us paper pencils and crayons.

7. Choose the correct word: ***Us*** or ***We***.

   '[ ] are going to play basketball', said Sam, Ben and Dan.

8. Write the adjective.

   Her drawing is better than yours.

   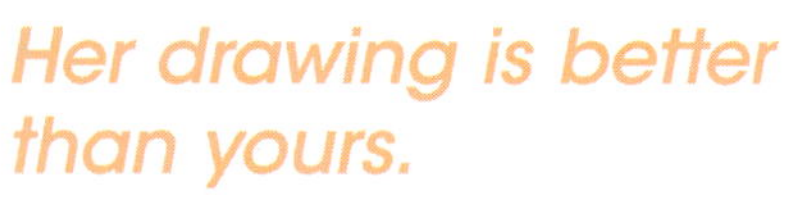

MY SCORE

Day 4

1. Write the jumbled word correctly.

   A whale is a geuh sea creature.

2. Write the missing letter(s). ***wh*** or ***w***

   The fire was nice and [ ]arm.

3. Write the words in alphabetical order.

   orange   pear   banana

4. Write ***ate*** or ***eight***.

   We [ ] spaghetti for dinner.

5. ***Answered*** and ***answering*** are made from the word [ ].

6. Write **.**, **!** or **?** in the box.

   I can't believe we won first place[ ]

7. Add one word: ***they*** or ***he***.

   Pat and Lee get into trouble because [ ] always push in.

8. Write ***or*** or ***but***.

   Do you want this [ ] can I have it?

MY SCORE

Day 5

1. Correct the spelling mistake.

   We will neva finish all this ice cream!

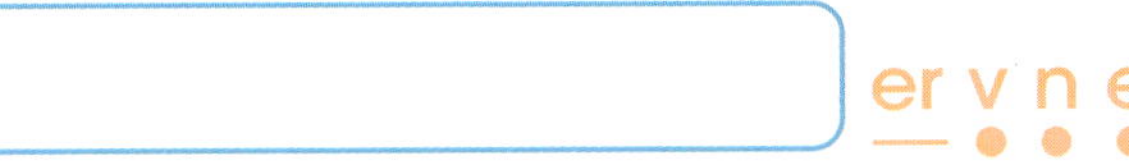

2. Write the missing letters. ***ork*** or ***alk***

   I had to w[ ] up a steep hill.

3. Circle the correct contraction (shortened word).

   wouldn't would'nt

4. Look at this sentence. Circle the mistake.

   I love going their on my holidays.

5. Write the singular of ***cities***.

6. Add two capital letters and a comma.

   i got books sweets and games for my birthday last april.

7. Choose the correct word.

   they them

   The children said [ ] were going to catch the train.

8. Write the adjective.

   The dusty carpet was hoovered by Dad.

Skill focus review

1. Correct the spelling mistake.

   I live far awaye from school.

   ay a w

2. Circle and write the verb group.

   Tina was talking too loudly.

3. Write the plural of ***sheep***.

4. Write ***there*** or ***their***.

   The man laughed loudly at [ ] joke.

5. Write the singular of ***butterflies***.

6. Add one comma.

   I bought my mum flowers chocolate and a nice card.

7. ***Copies*** and ***copied*** are made from the word [ ].

8. Circle present tense or past tense.

   Nessa is a fast runner.

   present past

Skill focus

What is editing?

Re-reading your sentences makes you a better writer.

It helps you see any mistakes you might have made. Then you can fix them.

This is called **editing**.

Some mistakes that people make are:

- Spelling mistakes:

  *I **liv** in the same street as my school.*

- Forgetting to use capital letters:

  ***m**y best friend and **i** have birthdays in **s**eptember.*

- Forgetting to use a full stop, question mark or exclamation mark:

  Where is the dog ☐

  I think he is under the tree ☐

- Adding an extra word:

  *The green grapes are in the **under** bowl.*

- Using the wrong word:

  *I use a paintbrush with my **write** hand.*

Practice questions

1. This sentence has two mistakes. Correct them.

   Oliver and bob like to eat spaghetti

2. Which word is not needed in the sentence?

   The black dog in ran past the car.

   ☐

Day 1

1. This sentence has two mistakes. Correct them.

   Is your birthday in march or April

2. Which word is not needed in the sentence?

   The girl dived safely up into the pool.

   ☐

3. Correct the spelling mistake.

   The deer was quic to move away.

   ☐ ck qu i

4. Write the words in alphabetical order.

   blocks cars dolls

   ☐ ☐ ☐

5. Circle the correct contraction (shortened word). ***it is*** =

   i'ts it's

6. Write ***it's*** or ***its***.

   The dog buried ☐ *bone.*

7. Write ***wood*** or ***would***.

   We get ☐ *from a tree.*

8. Write the better word: ***softly*** or ***loudly***.

   Dad sang ☐ *to help the baby fall asleep.*

MY SCORE ☐

Day 2

1. Look at this sentence. Circle the mistake.

   Jade and Brenda is friends.

2. Which word is not needed in the sentence?

   The clown walked under over to me.

3. Write the silent letter in this word.

   lamb

4. Write the plural of ***watch***.

5. Circle the two rhyming words.

   uncle   mother   brother

6. Write ***gone*** or ***went***.

   Everyone had ______ home by five o'clock.

7. Write ***pour*** or ***poor***.

   The ______ little girl had a thorn in her foot.

8. Circle the word that tells how the painter finished his work.

   The painter finished his work quickly.

   painter   work   quickly

MY SCORE

Day 3

1. This sentence has two mistakes. Correct them.

   My birthday is the second off june.

2. Which word is not needed in the sentence?

   The girl looked sadly up out the window.

3. Correct the spelling mistake.

   We were bisy tidying up.

   b u y s

4. Circle the word that comes first in alphabetical order.
   HINT: Use the second letter.

   plum   peach   pumpkin

5. Circle the correct contraction (shortened word). ***I have*** =

   Iv'e   I've

6. Write ***it's*** or ***its***.

   Mum said ______ time for tea.

7. Write ***wood*** or ***would***.

   I ______ like to sit there.

8. Write the better word: ***gently*** or ***greedily***.

   The boy ______ brushed the cat.

WEEK 25

Day 4

1. Look at this sentence. Circle the mistake.

   I hope I get the answer write.

2. Which word is not needed in the sentence?

   The boy is writing neatly down in his book.

3. Write the silent letter in this word.

   knew

4. Write the plural of ***dish***.

5. Circle the two rhyming words.

   strong sang belong

6. Write ***gone*** or ***went***.

   We ______ the wrong way and got lost.

7. Write ***pour*** or ***poor***.

   Be careful when you ______ the milk into the glass.

8. Circle the word that tells how the girl waved.

   The girl waved shyly to the lady.

   girl shyly lady

MY SCORE

Day 5

1. This sentence has two mistakes. Correct them.

   Mr taylor is my new neighbour?

2. Which word is not needed in the sentence?

   Yesterday, Mia is feeling sleepy today.

3. Correct the spelling mistake.

   The worta was dripping from the tap.

   er w a t

4. Circle the word that comes first in alphabetical order.

   kettle knife kite

5. Circle the correct contraction (shortened word). ***is not*** =

   isn't is'nt

6. Write ***it's*** or ***its***.

   The cat licked ______ paws.

7. Write ***wood*** or ***would***.

   I ______ like to go to the shop.

8. Write the better word: ***neatly*** or ***brightly***.

   Mum folded the clothes ______.

Skill focus

More conjunctions

Sentences are made from many different words. Some words join other words and sentences together. These are known as **conjunctions**.

The words ***and***, ***or*** and ***but*** are conjunctions.

They are used in the middle of sentences.

Some other conjunctions are:

These conjunctions are special because they can go at the start or in the middle of a sentence.

They are used to make sentences longer and more interesting.

If *you do your homework, then you can watch TV.*

I can't wait to go to the beach ***when*** *it is the weekend.*

I am sad ***because*** *I lost my favourite toy.*

Practice questions

1. Write ***because*** or ***and***.

   We worked hard all day ______ *we felt very tired.*

2. Use the conjunction (joining word) ***when*** or ***if***.

   Dad slowed down ______ *he got to the corner.*

Day 1

1. Use the conjunction (joining word) ***and*** or ***because*** to join the two parts of the sentence.

   I love pizza ______ *it is tasty.*

2. Circle the conjunction (joining word).

   We had to be quiet because the baby was asleep.

3. Correct the spelling mistake.

   Poot your dirty clothes in the wash.

   ______ u t P

4. Circle the word that comes first in alphabetical order.

   boat bus bike

5. Write ***saw*** or ***seen***.

   We ______ *a frog in the pond.*

6. Change the verb ***give*** so it makes sense in this sentence.

   Mum is ______ *me a present.*

7. Circle the verb.

   The white seagull flew away.

8. Write the word that is not needed.

   The extra dinosaurs once lived on Earth.

   ______

Day 2

1. Use the conjunction (joining word) ***When*** or ***If***.

   ______ *I work hard, I will get a nice treat.*

2. Circle the conjunction (joining word).

   We'll go outside when it stops raining.

3. Write the silent letter in this word.

   write ______

4. Add two letters to make the word say the opposite: ***true***.

   ______

5. Write ***has*** or ***have***.

   The boys ______ *gone to the tennis match.*

6. Change the verb ***move*** so it makes sense in this sentence.

   My best friend is ______ *to a new house.*

7. Circle present tense or past tense.

   Katie walks to school every day.

   present past

8. This sentence has two mistakes. Correct them.

   I can't wait for hour holiday at easter.

Day 3

1. Use the conjunction (joining word) ***because*** or ***and***.

   I did not go ______ *I was not feeling well.*

2. Circle the conjunction (joining word).

   I like art because it is fun.

3. Correct the spelling mistake.

   Your mum and dad are your parints.

   ______ p ar n t e s

4. Circle the word that comes first in alphabetical order.

   eye ear elbow

5. Write ***saw*** or ***seen***.

   Have you ______ *my new pencil?*

6. Change the verb ***snore*** so it makes sense in this sentence.

   Dad was ______ *on the chair.*

7. Circle the verb.

   Mum bought some fresh bread.

8. Write the word that is not needed.

   The biggest planet in the solar system is then called Jupiter.

   ______

Day 4

1. Use the conjunction (joining word) ***and*** or ***because***.

   Zoe went inside ______ *it was raining.*

2. Circle the conjunction (joining word).

   Our dog barks if the bell rings.

3. Write the silent letter in this word.

   comb ______

4. Add two letters to make the word say the opposite: ***pack***.

5. Write ***has*** or ***have***.

   That little boy ______ *nobody to play with.*

6. Change the verb ***chase*** so it makes sense in this sentence.

   The dog likes ______ *the cat.*

7. Circle present tense or past tense.

   The boys had walked home after school.

   present   past

8. This sentence has two mistakes. Correct them.

   Pat and Matt wood love to Eat a pizza.

Day 5

1. Use the conjunction (joining word) ***when*** or ***but***.

   We get a lift to school ______ *it is raining.*

2. Circle the conjunction (joining word).

   It was my party so I cut the cake.

3. Correct the spelling mistake.

   Mum sed we could have fish and chips for dinner.

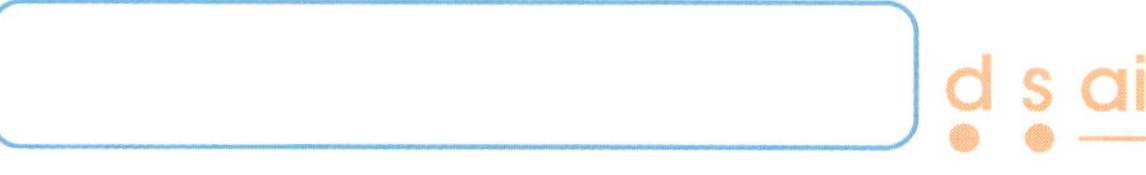

4. Circle the word that comes first in alphabetical order.

   skip   swim   slide

5. Write ***saw*** or ***seen***.

   I ______ *an elephant at the zoo.*

6. Change the verb ***shine*** so it makes sense in this sentence.

   The sun was ______ *brightly in the sky.*

7. Circle the verb.

   The goldfish leapt out of the tank.

8. Write the word that is not needed.

   The candles on over the birthday cake were pretty.

WEEK 26

Skill focus

Rules for adding endings (drop the *e*)

Sometimes we add letters to the end of words to make a new word.

smell + ing = smelling
talk + ed = talked
dust + y = dusty
strong + er = stronger
small + est = smallest

There are special rules for adding letters to the end of some words.

If the word ends with ***magic e***, we drop the ***e*** and add the ending.

shine	shine + ing = shining	shine + ed = shined	shine + y = shiny

Shine ends with ***magic e***.

Drop the ***e*** and add the ending.

cute	cute + er = cuter	cute + est = cutest

Cute ends wth ***magic e***.

Drop the ***e*** and add the ending.

Practice questions

Drop the ***e*** and add the ending to these words.

slime + y = ____________

ride + ing = ____________

Day 1

1. taste + y = ____________
2. Is the underlined word correct?

   yes ☐ no ☐

   The woman was wearing a <u>shiney</u> ring.
3. Write the jumbled word correctly.

   Dad is another word for <u>faethr</u>.

   ____
4. Write ***was*** or ***were***.

   A horse ____________ *eating grass.*
5. Write the opposite of ***good***.

   ____
6. Add the ending ***ful*** to ***care*** to make a new word.

   ____
7. This sentence has two mistakes. Correct them.

   When is the film Going to start.
8. Circle the conjunction (joining word).

   I like that pillow because it is soft.

Day 2

1. nice + er =

2. Is the underlined word correct?

   yes ☐ no ☐

   The writeer could not finish her book.

3. Add the missing silent letter.

   Do you ☐rite with your left hand?

4. Write the plural of ***city***.

5. Which word means the same as ***nearly***?

   late almost never

6. ***Careful*** and ***careless*** are made from what word?

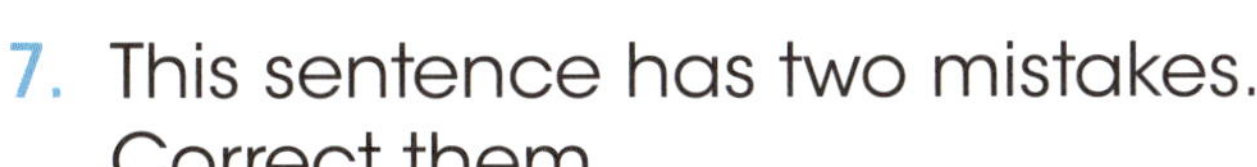

7. This sentence has two mistakes. Correct them.

   Noah have lots of muffins for the Party.

8. Write ***If*** or ***Because***.

   ☐ *we do good work, Mrs Murphy might give out stickers.*

Day 3

1. ride + ing =

2. Is the underlined word correct?

   yes ☐ no ☐

   The spider was slideing down the window.

3. Write the jumbled word correctly.

   We rode our bikes along the tpah.

4. Write ***was*** or ***were***.

   The horses ☐ *eating grass.*

5. Write the opposite of ***night***.

6. Add ***ly*** to ***bad*** to make a new word.

7. This sentence has two mistakes. Correct them.

   Abby and i are going to the playGround.

8. Circle the conjunction (joining word).

   Mrs Murphy smiled when I got the answer right.

WEEK 27

Day 4

1. fine + est =

2. Is the underlined word correct?

   yes ☐ no ☐

   My gran is the niceest of them all.

3. Add the missing silent letter.

   We heard a ☐ nock on the door.

4. Write the plural of ***story***.

5. Which word means the same as ***beginning***?

   winning starting running

6. ***Sadly*** and ***sadness*** are made from what word?

7. This sentence has two mistakes. Correct them.

   the cinema over there is closed

8. Write ***if*** or ***because***.

   Kirsten got into trouble ☐ she was talking.

Day 5

1. name + ed =

2. Is the underlined word correct?

   yes ☐ no ☐

   The children skateed through the park.

3. Write the jumbled word correctly.

   I ditre my hardest to finish the work.

4. Write ***was*** or ***were***.

   Kyle ☐ very excited when he saw his new bike.

5. Write the opposite of ***big***.

6. Add ***ness*** to ***sad*** to make a new word.

7. This sentence has two mistakes. Correct them.

   Bella and i went to the park

8. Circle the conjunction (joining word).

   I'll give it to you if you ask nicely.

Skill focus

Where is it?

Sentences are made from many different words. Some of these words tell us where people, places or things are. These are known as **prepositions**.

There are lots of other words that tell us where something is. They help make our sentences longer and more interesting.

The mouse was hiding.	*The mouse was hiding* ***behind a big cat.***

Practice questions

1. Circle the answer. Where is the boy?

   The boy is in his room.

2. Circle the answer. Where is the dog?

   The dog is on its bed.

Day 1

WEEK 28

1. Circle the answer. Where is the cat?

   The cat is on the windowsill.

2. Look at the picture. Read the sentence. Tick ***true*** or ***false***.

   The cat is on the windowsill.

   true ☐

   false ☐

3. Write the jumbled word correctly.

   Suddenly, it gnbae to rain.

4. rose + y =

5. Circle the word you can add to ***sun***.

   hot shine cloud

6. Change the verb ***crash*** so it makes sense in this sentence.

   The car ______ into the tree last night.

7. Circle the noun.

   The hospital was closed down.

8. Circle the conjunction (joining word).

   I'm going to be an astronaut when I grow up.

Day 2

1. Circle the answer. Where is the desk?

   The desk is between two cupboards.

2. Look at the picture. Read the sentence. Tick ***true*** or ***false***.

   The desk is between two cupboards.

   true ☐ false ☐

3. Add the missing silent letter.

   I brush and com☐ my own hair.

4. Add two letters to make the word say the opposite: ***tidy***.

   ☐

5. Write ***new*** or ***knew***.

   Jake and I have ☐ boots.

6. Change the verb ***give*** so it makes sense in this sentence.

   The baby just ☐ his mother a big smile.

7. Write the noun.

   Snakes can be very dangerous.

   ☐

8. Write the correct word. ***mine*** or ***yours***

   Here are my shoes.

   Those are ☐.

Day 3

1. Circle the answer. Where is the car?

   The car is in the garage.

2. Look at the picture. Read the sentence. Tick ***true*** or ***false***.

   The car is in the garage.

   true ☐ false ☐

3. Write the jumbled word correctly.

   Do you know what <u>mite</u> it starts?

   ☐

4. bake + ing = ☐

5. Circle the word you can add to ***end***.

   start day week

6. Change the verb ***ring*** so it makes sense in this sentence.

   She ☐ to say she would be late.

7. Circle the noun.

   Do you know where my gloves are?

8. Circle the conjunction (joining word).

   Mum says yes, but Dad says no.

Day 4

1. Circle the answer. Where is the plane?

   The plane is above the clouds.

2. Look at the picture. Read the sentence. Tick ***true*** or ***false***.

   The plane is above the clouds.

   true ☐ false ☐

3. Add the missing silent letter.

   She got the answer  *rong.*

4. Add two letters to make the word say the opposite: ***happy***.

5. Write ***new*** or ***knew***.

   I ______ *all the answers.*

6. Change the verb ***keep*** so it makes sense in this sentence.

   Milk is ______ *in the fridge.*

7. Write the noun.

   We went to London yesterday.

8. Write the correct word: ***theirs*** or ***ours***.

   They own this house.

   It is ______.

Day 5

1. Circle the answer. Where is the box?

   The box is under the table.

2. Look at the picture. Read the sentence. Tick ***true*** or ***false***.

   The box is under the table.

   true ☐ false 

3. Write the jumbled word correctly.

   My favourite season is tinwer.

4. bone + y =

5. Circle the word you can add to ***time***.

   clock long bed

6. Change the verb ***make*** so it makes sense in this sentence.

   Yesterday, Mum ______ *a cake for dessert.*

7. Circle the noun.

   That is a scary animal!

8. Circle the conjunction (joining word).

   We went for a swim because it was hot.

Skill focus

Rules for adding endings (double final consonant)

Sometimes we add letters to the end of words. This changes their meaning.

fast + er = faster	play + ing = playing
walk + ed = walked	salt + y = salty

There are special rules for adding letters to some words.

If the word ends with a vowel then a consonant, we double the last letter before adding the new ending.

<u>hop</u>	hop<u>ped</u>
Hop ends with a vowel then a consonant.	Double the last letter before adding ***ed***.

sw<u>im</u>	swi<u>mmer</u>
Swim ends with a vowel then a consonant.	Double the last letter before adding ***er***.

cl<u>ap</u>	cla<u>pping</u>
Clap ends with a vowel then a consonant.	Double the last letter before adding ***ing***.

f<u>un</u>	fu<u>nny</u>
Fun ends with a vowel then a consonant.	Double the last letter before adding ***y***.

Practice questions

Drop the ***e*** and add the ending to these words.

slime + y = ______

ride + ing = ______

Day 1

1. Add ***est*** to this word.

   hot______

2. Circle the correct word.

   sliped   slipped

   I ______ on a banana skin.

3. Correct the spelling mistake.

   We will <u>moove</u> into another house next week.

   ______ o e m v

4. Change the ***y*** to ***i*** before adding the ending.

   easy + ly = ______

5. Write ***was*** or ***were***.

   We ______ very excited when we saw the cake.

6. Correct this sentence.

   is mars the name of a planet

7. Circle the answer. Where is the fish?

   The fish is near the rock.

8. Write the adjective.

   Ivan saw an exciting film.

Day 2

1. Add ***ed*** to this word.

   drop ______

2. Circle the correct word.

   chatted   chated

   We ______ on the phone for hours.

3. Write the missing letters. ***al*** or ***el***

   A squirr ______ has a bushy tail.

4. Circle the word that comes second in alphabetical order.

   zip   zebra   zoo

5. Write the opposite of ***long***.

   ______

6. Add two capital letters and a comma.

   my sister maria bought a new dress hat and shoes.

7. Circle the answer. Where is the pencil?

   The pencil is under the book.

8. Is ***brave*** a noun or an adjective?

   The brave firefighter put out the fire.

   noun   adjective

Day 3

1. Add ***y*** to this word.

   spot ______

2. Circle the correct word.

   planing   planning

   We were ______ to go to the beach tomorrow.

3. Correct the spelling mistake.

   Would you like eny more to eat?

4. happy + ly = ______

5. Write ***was*** or ***were*** and ***to*** or ***two***.

   I ______ very happy when Dad said I could go ______ the party.

6. Correct this sentence.

   is your favourite subject at school art or science

7. Circle the answer. Where is the blue dress?

   The blue dress is in the wardrobe.

8. Write the adjective.

   The giraffe is the tallest animal in the world.

   ______

WEEK 29

Day 4

1. Add ***ing*** to this word.

   step

2. Circle the correct word.

   runny   runy

   I dipped my toast into the ______ egg.

3. Write the missing letters. ***al*** or ***el***

   A dolphin is a sea anim______.

4. Circle the word that comes second in alphabetical order.

   two   ten   three

5. Which word has the same meaning as ***fast***?

   run   quick   never

6. Add two capital letters and a comma.

   For christmas i would like a bike book and toy dinosaur.

7. Circle the answer.
   Where is the boat floating?

   The boat is floating on the water.

8. Is the word ***new*** a noun or an adjective?

   Dad is going to buy a new car.

   noun   adjective

Day 5

1. Add ***er*** to this word.

   fat

2. Circle the correct word.

   sader   sadder

   I feel ______ than I did yesterday.

3. Correct the spelling mistake.

   I have dun all my homework.

4. friendly + ness =

5. Write ***was*** or ***were*** and ***to*** or ***two***.

   Peter and Paul ______ talking about buying ______ new games.

6. Correct the two mistakes.

   did Beth get the write answer?

7. Circle the answer. Where is the bike?

   The bike is between the scooters.

8. Write the adjective.

   The cruel king never smiled.

Skill focus

A or an?

Sentences are made from many different words.

A and ***an*** are often used before a noun (naming word).

*Daniel read **a** book.*

A and ***an*** are used in the same way. Knowing when to use ***a*** or ***an*** can sometimes be tricky.

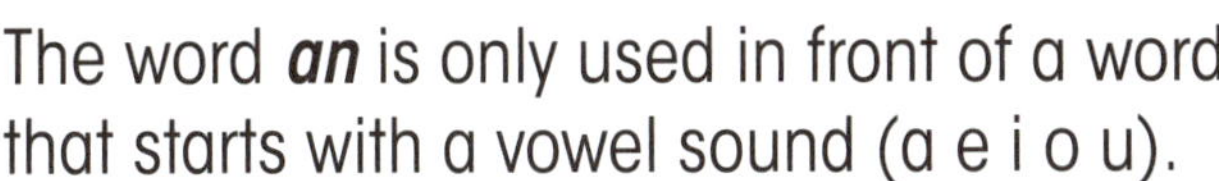

The word ***an*** is only used in front of a word that starts with a vowel sound (a e i o u).

*He has **an** apple.*

*I have **an** orange.*

Use ***a*** before words that start with a consonant.

Practice questions

1. Write ***a*** or ***an***.

   I made ☐ *spelling mistake.*

   He ate ☐ *apple.*

2. Is the underlined word correct?
   yes ☐ no ☐

   Would you like __an__ drink with your pizza?

Day 1

1. Write ***a*** or ***an***.

   Take ☐ *umbrella with you.*

2. Is the underlined word correct?

   yes ☐ no ☐

   Would you like to go for __an__ ride to the library?

3. Correct the spelling mistake.

   I went to the park __bifore__ school.

   ☐ ore f b e

4. swim + ing = ☐

5. Write ***know*** or ***no***.

   The opposite of yes is ☐.

6. Circle the correct contraction (shortened word).

   what's what's

7. Write the word ***yourself*** or ***myself***.

   I wanted to do it by ☐.

8. Circle the two words that make the verb group.

   The dog is digging a big hole.

WEEK 30

Day 2

1. Write ***a*** or ***an***.

orange.

2. Is the underlined word correct?

yes ☐ no ☐

How much does a packet of biscuits cost?

3. Write the missing letters. ***el*** or ***le***

The door hand☐ was loose.

4. cry + ing =

5. Write ***war*** or ***wore***.

The opposite of peace is ☐.

6. Correct this sentence.

the butterfly had yellow and black wings

7. Look at the picture. Read the sentence. Tick ***true*** or ***false***.

The car is in the tunnel.

true ☐ false ☐

8. Write the better conjunction (joining word): ***so*** or ***because***.

That shirt needs to be washed

it is dirty.

MY SCORE

Day 3

1. Write ***a*** or ***an***.

Please could I have ☐ drink?

2. Is the underlined word correct?

yes ☐ no ☐

My sister is a excellent dancer.

3. Correct the spelling mistake.

I watch TV at nite time.

t igh n

4. flat + er = ☐

5. Write ***know*** or ***no***.

Do you ☐ what to do?

6. Circle the correct contraction (shortened word).

that's tha'ts

7. Choose the correct word: ***she*** or ***her***.

My sister is only two, so Mum helps ☐ to cut up her food.

8. Circle the two words that make the verb group.

The kitten was playing with a ball.

MY SCORE

Day 4

1. Write ***a*** or ***an***.

tomato

2. Is the underlined word correct?

yes ▢ no ▢

I would like <u>an</u> apple for my lunch.

3. Write the missing letters. ***le*** or ***el***

Please hang up your wet tow▢.

4. dry + ing = ▢

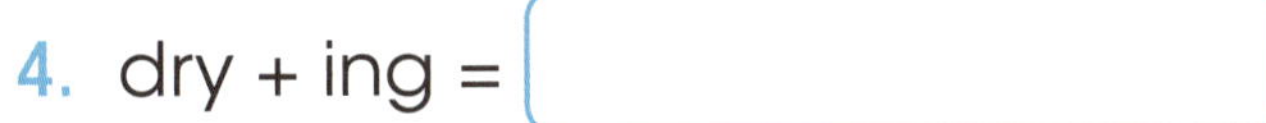

5. Write ***war*** or ***wore***.

Dad ▢ jeans and a T-shirt.

6. Correct this sentence.

do you know who has my shoes

7. Look at the picture. Read the sentence. Tick ***true*** or ***false***.

The dog is behind the tree.

true ▢ false ▢

8. Write the better conjunction (joining word): ***so*** or ***but***.

It was raining, ▢ we got wet walking home.

MY SCORE

Day 5

1. Write ***a*** or ***an***.

Do you own ▢ bike?

2. Is the underlined word correct?

yes ▢ no ▢

We saw <u>an</u> elephant at the zoo.

3. Correct the spelling mistake.

What is your <u>naim</u>?

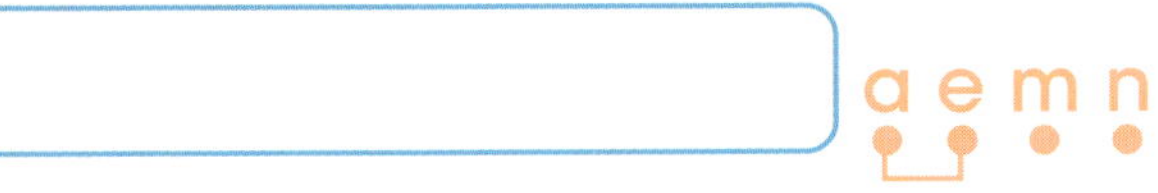

a e m n

4. run + y = ▢

5. Write ***wait*** or ***weight***.

The ▢ of a brick is more than that of a pebble.

6. Circle the correct contraction (shortened word).

don't do'nt

7. Write the better word: ***ourselves*** or ***themselves***.

Sarah and Kate like to play the game ▢.

8. Circle the two words that make the verb group.

Matt has lost his ruler and pencil.

MY SCORE

WEEK 30

Skill focus

Rules for adding endings (change *f* to *v*)

A **plural** is a word used to show more than one of something.

When words end in ***f***, there are special rules for making a plural.

Change the ***f*** to ***v*** then add ***es***.

Practice questions

1. Is the underlined word correct?
   yes ☐ no ☐
   Cut the apple into two halves.

2. Write the plural of these words.
   one calf, two ________
   one thief, two ________

Day 1

1. Is the underlined word correct?
   yes ☐ no ☐
   My mum owns lots of scarfs.

2. The plural of ***scarf*** is ________.

3. Correct the spelling mistake.
   I was the larst person in the line.
   ________ a s t l

4. Circle the word that comes first in alphabetical order.
   sand shell seagull

5. Write ***not*** or ***knot***.
   I tied a ________ *in my shoelace.*

6. Write the word that is not needed.
   The artist didn't painted a beautiful picture.
   ____

7. Write ***a*** or ***an***.
   Would you like to go for ________ *walk?*

8. Circle the word that tells how the child walked.
   The child walked quietly to the classroom.

Day 2

1. Is the underlined word correct?

   yes ☐ no ☐

   The baker sells many different loafs of bread.

2. The plural of ***loaf*** is ________.

3. Write the missing letters. ***al*** or ***il***.

   She got a med____ for coming first.

4. Circle the word that can be built from ***sweep***.

   sweepes sweeping sweeply

5. Write ***wait*** or ***weight***.

   We had to ________ a long time before we got served.

6. Correct this sentence.

   please don't touch there paintings

7. Write ***a*** or ***an***.

   ____ ice cream

8. Circle the answer.
   Where is the bag?

   The bag is on the hook.

Day 3

1. Is the underlined word correct?

   yes ☐ no ☐

   My favourite story is about elfs and a shoemaker.

2. The plural of ***elf*** is ________.

3. Correct the spelling mistake.

   I like dogs and I allso like cats.

4. Circle the word that comes first in alphabetical order.

   custard cake cookies

5. Write ***not*** or ***knot***.

   The baby would ________ go to sleep.

6. Correct the two mistakes.

   Grace dosen't like to sit beside philip.

7. Write ***a*** or ***an***.

   I have ____ older sister.

8. Circle the word that tells how the boy waited.

   The boy waited bravely for the doctor.

WEEK 31

WEEK 31

Day 4

1. Is the underlined word correct?

   yes ☐ no ☐

   The leafs were starting to fall from the tree.

2. The plural of ***leaf*** is ________.

3. Write the missing letters. ***al*** or ***il***

   My lead penc____ is blunt.

4. Circle the word that can be built from ***wait***.

   waitful waitly waited

5. Circle the two rhyming words.

   said ready bread

6. Write the word that is not needed.

   The website had a great sale time on shirts and jumpers.

   ____

7. Write ***a*** or ***an***.

   ____ cookie

8. Circle the answer. Where is the balloon?

   The balloon is above the presents.

Day 5

1. Is the underlined word correct?

   yes ☐ no ☐

   The wolfs howled at the moon.

2. The plural of ***wolf*** is ________.

3. Correct the spelling mistake.

   Did you leav your hat at home?

   ________ ea ve l

4. Circle the word that comes last in alphabetical order.

   apple avocado apricot

5. Circle the word that does not rhyme.

   four shore flour

6. Correct this sentence.

   mum and i hung out the shirts and jeans

7. Write ***a*** or ***an***.

   I had ____ egg for breakfast today.

8. Circle the word that tells how the wind blew.

   The wind blew calmly.

Day 1

1. Correct the spelling mistake.

   What do you <u>wont</u> for your birthday?

2. Write the missing letters. ***ch*** or ***tch***

   Whi ____ sock is yours?

3. Circle the word that comes last in alphabetical order.

   what's we've won't

4. Write ***threw*** or ***through***.

   Josh ____ the ball so far that it rolled into the bushes.

5. The plural of ***thief*** is ____.

6. Look at this sentence. Circle the mistake.

   The children was laughing at the joke.

7. Circle the conjunction (joining word).

   We'll go shopping when Mum's ready.

8. Circle and write the verb group.

   We are building a sandcastle.

Day 2

1. Write the jumbled word correctly.

   We don't have to go to school <u>odtay</u>.

2. Write the missing letters. ***ge*** or ***dge***

   Put the flowerpot on the le____.

3. Circle the word that can be built from ***mix***.

   mixful mixly mixing

4. Write ***road*** or ***rode***.

   I ____ my bike to school.

5. Circle the correct contraction (shortened word).

   hel'l he'll

6. Add a capital letter and two commas.

   you will need paper scissors glue and coloured pencils.

7. Write ***a*** or ***an***.

   I went on ____ ride at the beach.

8. Circle the noun.

   Some pretty parrots were squawking loudly.

WEEK 32

WEEK 32

Day 3

1. Correct the spelling mistake.

   We walk to school evry day.

   v e er y

2. Write the missing letters. ***ch*** or ***tch***

   Dad used a ma ____ to light the fire.

3. Circle the word that comes last in alphabetical order.

   pink   purple   plum

4. Write ***threw*** or ***through***.

   A tunnel was cut ____ the mountain.

5. The plural of ***hoof*** is ____.

6. Circle the word that is not needed.

   The taxi driver drove us crazy to the airport.

7. Circle the conjunction (joining word).

   I had my hair cut because it had grown too long.

8. Circle the verb group.

   The school bus has arrived on time.

MY SCORE

Day 4

1. Write the jumbled word correctly.

   Are you urse you know the way?

2. Write the missing letters. ***ge*** or ***dge***

   He pinned the ba ____ to his jacket.

3. Circle the word that can be built from ***long***.

   longly   longest   longes

4. Write ***road*** or ***rode***.

   Drivers need to drive carefully on the ____.

5. Circle the correct contraction (shortened word).

   she'll   shel'l

6. Add two capital letters and a comma.

   i would like a chocolate caramel and peanut butter egg for easter.

7. Write ***a*** or ***an***.

   There was ____ animal hiding in the bushes.

8. Is ***picnic*** a noun or a verb?

   Our family had a picnic at the river.

MY SCORE

Day 5

1. Correct the spelling mistake.

   I am betta than my sister at drawing.

   er tt b e

2. Write the missing letters. ***ch*** or ***tch***

   Our pet rabbit lives in a hu______.

3. Circle the word that comes last in alphabetical order.

   television table trampoline

4. Write ***threw*** or ***through***.

   We walk ______ the park to get home.

5. The plural of ***half*** is ______.

6. Correct this sentence.

   Dad had to weight for a long time for oliver to come home.

7. Circle the conjunction (joining word).

   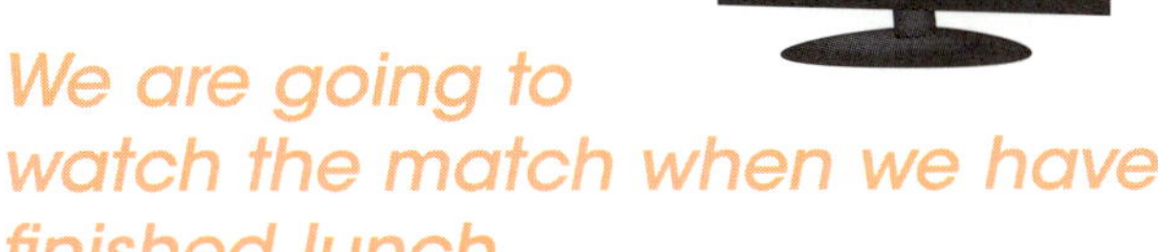

   We are going to watch the match when we have finished lunch.

8. Circle the verb group.

   Jack is talking in the room.

Skill focus review

1. Correct the spelling mistake.

   My naim is Jenny.

2. Add ***ing*** to the end of ***smile***.

3. chat + ing = ______

4. one scarf, two ______

5. Use the conjunction (joining word) ***if*** or ***because***.

   You can have a muffin ______ you say please.

6. Circle the answer. Where is the plane?

   The plane is above the houses.

7. Write ***a*** or ***an***.

   Can we go on ______ holiday soon?

8. Write the word that is not needed.

   The computer was repaired by the kind caretaker tomorrow.

WEEK 32

NOTES

NOTES

NOTES